Biblical Greek

Book 2

Nouns and Cases

Biblical Greek

Book 2

Nouns and Cases

James T. and Lisa M. Cummins

———————

But the goal of our instruction is love from a pure heart
and a good conscience and a sincere faith.
1 Timothy 1:5, NASB

———————

Table of Contents

continued, next page

Introduction

Welcome to the second book of the *Biblical Greek* series. It's our hope that you will thoroughly enjoy the chance to learn the very words of scripture as they are recorded in the Greek of the New Testament. It might help to know that we, the authors of this series, pray over you and all the readers who use these books. We pray for your success, not merely academically, but in areas of the *heart*. Our hope is that you enjoy a prosperous life in obedience to God's Word. After all, a closer, more obedient walk with God is the whole point of learning the Greek of the scriptures.

We realize what you're up against (spiritually speaking) as you take on Book 2. This is one reason we make a habit of praying over our readers regularly. Please allow us to join with you in prayer right now, asking God's help in your endeavor to learn Greek. *"Jesus, thank You for this chance to study the Greek of Your scriptures. Please help me, by Your great grace, as I attempt to learn."* "Amen!" we say in agreement!

What will you learn in this book? Well, you've already completed Book 1, in which you learned the Greek alphabet, along with the "top twenty nouns" in singular form, in the nominative case. This book will pick up from there, introducing **other nouns, other cases** besides the nominative case, **plural forms of the nouns**, and the Greek **article**. We'll do our best to keep the explanations as simple and brief as possible. We'll also try to keep the book lighthearted, with plenty of jokes, puzzles and cartoons along the way. No reason not to have fun while you learn, right?

By the end of this short workbook, you'll know the case forms of more than twenty New Testament nouns, and you'll understand the grammatical purpose of each case – a key step in the journey toward learning to translate scripture for yourself. Won't that be wonderful? So, keep your eyes on the prize, and ask for God's grace while you study. He promises *always* to help you through it.

> *"...and reaching forward to what lies ahead, I press on toward the goal*
> *for the prize of the upward call of God in Christ Jesus."*
> *– Philippians 3:13b-14*

Lesson 1: How Cases Work

In Book 1 of this series, you memorized the top twenty most frequently used nouns in the Greek New Testament. If you'll recall, we told you that the form (i.e., spelling) of each noun that we were teaching you was only *one* of the noun's many forms. The form of a Greek noun varies, all depending on its **case – the grammatical function of that word as it is being used in a sentence.** All twenty nouns that you learned in Book 1 have several different spellings, all depending on which case (grammatical role) they are performing in a particular sentence. To make things easier for you at the time, we only showed you *one particular case* of those nouns: the *nominative* case, which is defined as "when the noun is functioning as the *subject* of a Greek sentence."

Of course, the nominative case is not the *only* case in existence. There are actually **five cases** in Biblical Greek. Each case represents a different scenario in which the noun plays a unique grammatical role in a sentence.

This lesson will focus only on *two* of the cases. We don't want to overwhelm you. It's best to let you get your feet wet very slowly. You are familiar with the spellings of the twenty nouns in one form, the *nominative* case. So, this lesson will gradually introduce the spellings for the *accusative* case, too. But first, we need to explain what these two cases are and how they work.

To do that, we'll start off easy, with simple illustrations from English sentences. The following discussion might seem familiar to you, because we are repeating much of it from Book 1. A little repetition never hurt anyone!

Easy illustrations from English sentences

Greek nouns get different suffixes tacked on to them (and therefore slightly change spellings), *depending on their grammatical function in a sentence.* Each grammatical function is called a **case**.

For example, if a noun is functioning as the **subject** of a sentence (the person or thing *doing* the action), the noun is said to be in the **nominative case**. English examples of words functioning as the **subject** are underlined and bolded in the sentences below:

> The **man** threw the ball.
> The **ball** hit the vase.

On the other hand, if a noun is functioning as the **direct object** of the verb (the person or thing *receiving* the action), it is said to be in the **accusative case**. English examples of words functioning as the **direct object** are underlined and bolded in the sentences below:

> The man threw the **ball**.
> The ball hit the **vase**.

Did you notice that the word "ball" didn't change spellings between the two sentences as it changed functions from direct object to a subject? Of *course* it didn't! That would be weird! But, that's where Greek is so different from English. In Greek, there *would* be a different set of letters added to the end of the word, all depending on whether that word was in the *nominative* or *accusative* case.

Wait a minute, though. Before we get all "high and mighty" about how much nicer and simpler English is than Greek, let's all eat a huge piece of humble pie and take a good look at the following English examples of case forms in which the spellings *do* change.

Easy English examples of case forms

English nouns don't change forms willy-nilly based on grammatical function like Greek nouns do. Thank goodness for that. But, would you be surprised to learn that English *pronouns* can, and often do, change forms depending on grammatical function? Therefore, English *does* have case forms, but just for pronouns, not for nouns. For example, consider the following sentences about one cheerleader (1) tossing a second cheerleader (2) high into the air.

The **cheerleader** tossed the second **cheerleader** high into the air.
     1   2

As any English speaker would reasonably expect, the noun "cheerleader" did *not* suddenly change spellings willy-nilly simply because in case 1 it was acting as the *subject* of the sentence and in case 2 is was acting as an *object*. (Greek nouns, of course *would* change spellings, but not English nouns). However, take a look at this sentence, in which we replaced the nouns with *pronouns:*

She tossed **her** high into the air.
 1   2

Notice how those pronouns actually changed their forms (spellings), all depending on their case. The pronoun that means "a singular female person" is spelled "she" only when it is filling the role of *subject* (1). That same pronoun changes its spelling to "her" when it is filling the role of *object* (2).

Are there any other examples of case forms in English? Here are a few:

He tossed **him** high into the air.   ("he" = subject   "him" = object)
They tossed **them** high into the air.   ("they" = subject "them" = object)
Who tossed **whom** high into the air? ("who" = subject "whom" = object)

The nominative case

The **nominative** case is defined as **the case that the subject is in**. To figure out which word is the subject of a sentence, you can try a simple "question test." Ask yourself: **Who** or **what** is **doing the activity**? Try this test now on our simple sentence examples from earlier. We have underlined the **subjects**:

> The **man** threw the ball.   (Who threw? The **man**.)
>
> The **ball** hit the vase.   (What hit? The **ball**.)

If these had been Greek sentences, the underlined words would be in the **nominative** case, and their spellings would have the kind of endings which are used for the nominative case.

Why not just look for the first noun in a sentence and assume it is the subject? Because grammar doesn't really work that way. In English, subjects *usually* appear toward the beginning of a sentence and before the verb, but that's not *always* the situation. Sometimes, they can appear at the *end* of a sentence and *after* the verb. To illustrate, use the "question test" on the examples below and see if you can identify the subject of each sentence. **Underline each subject now.**

> "Yes!" shouted the boy.
>
> Even more important is the law.
>
> Into danger rode the knight.

Did you underline *boy, law* and *knight*? If so, you were correct. These examples really demonstrate how **case is *not* determined by word's position in a sentence. Case is *only* determined by the grammatical function of a word.** In fact, each of the sentences above could easily have been written in a completely different order, further proving that the subjects really are *boy, law* and *knight*. Below, we underlined the subject of each sentence. Then we rewrote the sentence in a different order.

Original sentence:	"Yes!" shouted the **boy.**
Rewritten sentence:	The **boy** shouted, "Yes!"
Question test:	Who shouted?
Answer:	The **boy**.

Original sentence:	Even more important is the **law.**
Rewritten sentence:	The **law** is even more important.
Question test:	What is?
Answer:	The **law**.

Original sentence:	Into danger rode the **knight.**
Rewritten sentence:	The **knight** rode into danger.
Question test:	Who rode?
Answer:	The **knight**.

When the verb is not an action type of verb

Occasionally, you'll see a sentence that doesn't have an action verb in it, but instead uses an equative verb like "is" or "are."   An *equative* verb simply *equates* the subject of the sentence with something else. If that "something else" happens to be another noun, then that other noun is *also* in the nominative case.   Here are some examples of sentences containing equative verbs in which we underlined all words that are in the nominative case.

<u>I</u> am a <u>**boy.**</u>
<u>**Matthew**</u> is a <u>**man.**</u>
<u>**Jesus**</u> is <u>**God.**</u>

This idea of nominatives in both the subject and the predicate isn't something you have to memorize right now. It's just something we wanted to mention, because the Greek of the Bible uses these equatives a *lot*. Don't sweat it. You'll absorb this idea naturally, just by doing the exercises in this book.

What if I'm really bad at all this grammar stuff?

Right about now, more than half of all students will have broken out in a cold sweat.   That's because more than half of us really struggle with grammar. Many of you are thinking, *Oh, no! Will I really have to be able to identify the subject of a sentence in order to go any further with Greek?*

We have great news for you! *Most of the time, you won't have to identify the subject of a sentence in order to learn Greek,* because *Greek will do the identifying <u>for</u> you!* Here's what we mean: the Greek words themselves have special ending letters that were purposely put there to tell you exactly what their cases are. After we teach you those special endings, you will rarely have to figure out a word's case by yourself. The answers will usually be right there in front of your nose.

On the next few pages, we're going to show you some examples of this great feature of Greek, and we think that you will be delighted! But first, we will need to explain the accusative case.

The accusative case

The **accusative** case is defined as **the case that the direct object is in**. To figure out which word is the direct object, you can use another "question test." Ask yourself: **who** or **what** is **receiving the action**? Returning to our simple sentences, try using this question to determine the direct object. We have underlined the direct objects:

The man threw the <u>**ball**</u>.   (What's being thrown? the <u>**ball**</u>.)
The ball hit the <u>**vase**</u>.   (What's being hit? the <u>**vase**</u>.)

Nominative and accusative case forms in scripture

The best way for you to understand case forms is to see them in action. We're going to show you three different scripture passages containing three of the top twenty nouns you memorized from Book 1. You'll soon recognize that all the nouns we have chosen for these examples happen to be from your list of **masculine** nouns, and they are all **singular**.

The examples are actual phrases from the Greek New Testament. Since we haven't taught you all the vocabulary from these phrases yet, we included brief definitions underneath each Greek word, just for your convenience. **Please don't try to learn any new vocabulary;** that will only distract you from the objective of this lesson. Instead, **please focus *only* on the words highlighted in gray.** Read each passage carefully and then turn the page; we'll explain each passage in more detail there.

Passage 1 *from 1 John 2*

... ὁ κόσμος παράγεται...
the   world   is passing away

... the **world** is passing away...
1 John 2:17

Μὴ ἀγαπᾶτε τὸν κόσμον...
not   love   the   world

Love not the **world**...
1 John 2:15

Passage 2 *from Romans 7*

...νόμος ἅγιος...
law   [is] holy

... the **law** is holy...
Romans 7:12

...γινώσκουσιν γὰρ νόμον λαλῶ...
to those knowing   indeed   law   I speak

...to those knowing indeed the **law** I speak...
Romans 7:1

Passage 3 *from Mark 13*

καὶ παραδώσει ἀδελφὸς ἀδελφὸν εἰς θάνατον...
and   shall deliver up   brother   brother   to   death

And **brother** shall deliver up **brother** to death...
Mark 13:12

We're guessing the first thing you noticed was the unusual spelling of the *second* instance of each gray-highlighted word. Rather than having the spellings you learned in Book 1 which end with the letter *sigma* (ς), the latter instances all end with the letter *nu* (ν).

Why is that? It's because the latter instances all represent situations in which the word is in a *different case*. In each latter instance, the word is literally performing a different grammatical role, or function, than it's performing in the first instance.

Using your new knowlege about the nominative and accusative cases, see if you can figure out which instance is demonstrating which case. Let's look at the passages more closely.

Passage 1 *from 1 John 2*

... ὁ	κόσμος	παράγεται...
the	*world*	*is passing away*

... the **world** is passing away...
1 John 2:17

Ask yourself: is the word "world" here acting as the *subject* or as a *direct object*? Ask: Who or what is *doing* the activity of passing away? Answer: The world. So, the *world* is the *subject*. Therefore, the Greek word κόσμος is in the **nominative case**. That is the reason the Greek language spells it here so it ends with a **sigma**.

Μὴ	ἀγαπᾶτε	τὸν	κόσμον...
not	*love*	*the*	*world*

Love not the **world**...
1 John 2:15

Ask yourself: is the word "world" here acting as the *subject* or as a *direct object*? Ask: Who or what would be *receiving* the activity of the loving? Answer: The world. So, the *world* is the *direct object*. Therefore, the Greek word κόσμον is in the **accusative case**. That is the reason the Greek language spells it here so it ends with a **nu**.

Passage 2 *from Romans 7*

...νόμος	ἅγιος...
law	*[is] holy*

... the **law** is holy...
Romans 7:12

Here, the word *law* is acting as the *subject* of the sentence. Therefore, the Greek word νόμος is in the **nominative case** and ends with a **sigma**.

...γινώσκουσιν	γὰρ	νόμον	λαλῶ...
to those knowing	*indeed*	*law*	*I speak*

...to those knowing indeed the **law** I speak...
Romans 7:1

Here, the word *law* is acting as the *direct object* of the sentence. It is receiving the action of being "known." Therefore, the Greek word νόμον is in the **accusative case** and ends with a **nu**.

καὶ παραδώσει ἀδελφὸς ἀδελφὸν εἰς θάνατον...
and   shall deliver up   brother   brother   to   death

And **brother** shall deliver up **brother** to death...
Mark 13:12

Here, the first instance of the word *brother* is acting as the *subject* of the sentence. That brother is the one who is doing the "delivering up." Therefore, the Greek word ἀδελφός is in the **nominative case** and ends with a **sigma**. However, the second instance of the word *brother* is *receiving* the action of "being delivered up." Therefore, the Greek word ἀδελφόν is in the **accusative case** and ends with a **nu**.

Case endings tell you the answers

What's really great about Greek is this: once you learn which endings go with which cases (plus learn all the case forms for the definite article – we'll be teaching you *that* trick pretty soon), then you will always be able to discern the grammatical role of each word in the sentence! No sentence diagramming required! It's a beautiful system, really. By the way, the technical term for the unique ending letters on cases is – unsurprisingly – "**case endings.**"

We do want to remind you that the only examples you've seen so far are nouns which happen to be **masculine** and **singular**. There's actually a different set of case endings for plurals, not to mention feminine nouns and neuter nouns. We'll show you those in later lessons.

What's a "stem"?

Before we go any further, we need to define an important concept in Greek called the *stem* of a word. In linguistics, a **stem is the basic part of the word to which suffixes and prefixes are attached.** In our Greek examples of the three passages, the stems were the parts of the words to which we attached the case ending of either sigma (ς) or nu (ν).

Do we have stems in English? Sure. The words **friend**s, **friend**ship, un**friend**ly and be**friend** all have the stem *friend*, to which various suffixes and/or prefixes have been attached. The stem of a word holds the basic meaning. That meaning carries through, no matter what types of prefixes or suffixes get added to it.

On the next page, we'll take a closer look at the stems of the three Greek words we just studied in the scripture passages.

Identifying stems and case endings in our examples

Here are enlargements of your vocabulary words from the three passages, in both nominative and accusative case forms. We've written their stems in outlined lettering and their case endings in solid lettering.

κόσμος

world, universe
nominative case

κόσμον

world, universe
accusative case

νόμος

law, principle
nominative case

νόμον

law, principle
accusative case

ἀδελφός*

brother
nominative case

ἀδελφόν

brother
accusative case

Once you know what you're looking for, it's fairly easy to discern the case endings from the stems, isn't it?

---

*You may have noticed that, on *this* page, the accents on the words ἀδελφός and ἀδελφόν are *acute* accents, while in the context of the scripture on the preceding page, they were both *grave*. Isolated words that would ordinarily have acute accents can undergo a change to a grave accent once they are placed into the context of a sentence. There is a rule that certain acute accents get changed to grave whenever the word is followed by a punctuation mark or by certain other words (like words which lack their own accent marks). Please don't worry about learning the rules for accent mark changes right now. Accent changes happen frequently and for a wide variety of reasons, but they *don't* affect a word's grammatical function (its case). Your only job right now is to focus on the case ending letters.

Case endings apply to proper nouns, too

It's important to know that case endings apply to proper nouns, too, such as the Greek names for Peter and Paul. Note the nominative and accusative case endings on those two names here.

...Πέτρος περιεπάτησεν ἐπὶ τὰ ὕδατα...   "**Peter** walked on the water" (Matt. 14:29)

καὶ ἀπέστειλεν Πέτρον...   "and he sent **Peter**" (Luke 22:8)

...ὁ δὲ Παῦλος ἔφη πρὸς αὐτούς...   "but **Paul** said to them" (Acts 16:37)

... καὶ λιθάσαντες τὸν Παῦλον...   "and having stoned **Paul**" (Acts 14:19)

Other spelling patterns do exist in Greek

At the risk of being overly repetitious on this point, let us again emphasize that the spelling pattern for the case endings on the previous page are true for *many* Greek nouns, but certainly not for *all* of them. They are true for many masculine singular nouns having a particular stem spelling. Other Greek nouns follow different spelling patterns for their nominative and accusative case endings. The pattern they follow depends on both their genders and the spellings of their stems.

Don't worry about those other patterns right now. Rest assured, by the end of this book, you will have learned most of the frequently used patterns. We didn't want to make this first lesson overwhelming by introducing them all at once.

Look, Jane!
Me swing on vine!

No, dear. You need to use the *nominative case*, remember? It's "*I* swing, not *me* swing."

Tarzan's grammatical cases always were a bit dicey.

Exercise 1.1 – Choose the Correct Case Form

Below are phrases from the Greek New Testament which include masculine nouns from your Top Twenty Nouns list. A choice of two case forms is given in each set of parentheses. **Circle the correct form that completes each sentence.** Hint: It's easiest to use the complete translated English verse to determine the grammatical role of the word. Remember that the **nominative** case is for the **subject** of a sentence (the person or thing which is doing the action), while the **accusative** is for the **direct object** (the person or thing which is receiving the action). An answer key with explanations follows the exercise.

1 ... Ὁ (Κύριος / Κύριον) αὐτοῦ χρείαν ἔχει ...

    the   *Lord*   *of it*   *need*   *has*

"If anyone asks you, 'Why are you doing this?' say, 'The **Lord** needs him;' and immediately he will send him back here" (Mark 11:3).

2 Πνεῦμα ὁ (Θεός / Θεόν) ...

 spirit   *[is]*   *God*

"**God** is spirit, and those who worship him must worship in spirit and truth" (John 4:24).
Hint: The word "is" acts as an equative verb in this situation. See page 14 for a refresher on this.

3 καὶ ἀγαπήσεις (Κύριος / Κύριον) τὸν (Θεός / Θεόν) σου...

 and   *you shall love*   *[the] Lord*   *the*   *God*   *of you*

"...and you shall love the **Lord** your **God** with all your heart, and with all your soul, and with all your mind, and with all your strength..." (Mark 12:30)

4 ...Οὐκ οἶδα τὸν (ἄνθρωπος / ἄνθρωπον).

   not   *I know*   *the*   *man*

"Again he denied it with an oath, 'I don't know the **man**'" (Matthew 26:72).

5 ...Οὐκ ἐπ' ἄρτῳ μόνῳ ζήσεται ὁ (ἄνθρωπος / ἄνθρωπον) ...

   not   *by*   *bread*   *alone*   *shall live*   *the*   *man*

"But he answered, 'It is written, **Man** shall not live by bread alone, but by every word that proceeds out of the mouth of God'" (Matthew 4:4).

Exercise 1.1, *continued*

6 ...καὶ ἐλάλουν τὸν (λόγος / λόγον)...

     and   they spoke   the   word

"When they had prayed, the place was shaken where they were gathered together. They were all filled with the Holy Spirit, and they spoke the **word** of God with boldness" (Acts 4:31).

7 ...Ἐν ἀρχῇ ἦν ὁ (λόγος / λόγον)...

     in   beginning   was   the   word

"In the beginning was the **Word**, and the Word was with God, and the Word was God" (John 1:1).

8 ...ὑμεῖς δὲ οὐχ οὕτως ἐμάθετε τὸν (Χριστός / Χριστόν)...

     you   however   not   this way   learned   -   Christ

"But you did not learn **Christ** that way..." (Ephesians 4:20)

9 ...ὁ (Χριστὸς / Χριστὸν) μένει εἰς τὸν αἰῶνα...

     the   Christ   abides   to   the   age

"The multitude answered him, 'We have heard out of the law that the **Christ** remains forever. How do you say, "The Son of Man must be lifted up?" Who is this Son of Man?'" (John 12:34)

10 ...σὺ ὁ ποιήσας τὸν (οὐρανὸς / οὐρανὸν)...

     you   who   made   the   heaven

"When they heard it, they lifted up their voice to God with one accord, and said, 'O Lord, you are God, who made the **heaven**, the earth, the sea, and all that is in them...'" (Acts 4:24)

Answers 1.1

1. Κύριος. The *nominative* form is the correct choice, because the "Lord" is the *subject*, the one who is doing the "needing."

2. Θεός. The *nominative* form is the correct choice, because the equative verb "is" tells what God "is", which is "spirit." Equative verbs set a subject and another noun equal to each other, so that both nouns end up in the nominative case. See top of page 14 for a full explanation.

3. Κύριον, Θεόν. The *accusative* forms are the correct choices for both words, because both "Lord" and "God" are *direct objects*, which *receive* the action of the verb, which is "love."

4. ἄνθρωπον. The *accusative* form is the correct choice, because "man" is the *direct object*. "Man" is not the person who is doing the "knowing;" he is the person who is being known.

5. ἄνθρωπος. The *nominative* form is the correct choice, because "man" is the *subject*, the one who is doing the "living." Note the unusual order of the words in the original Greek, so that the subject was positioned at the very end. Don't let the word order fool you.

6. λόγον. The *accusative* form is the correct choice, because "word" is the *direct object*. "Word" is the thing that was "spoken" by the believers.

7. λόγος. The *nominative* form is the correct choice, because "word" is the *subject* of the sentence, even though it appears after the verb "was." The same sentence could easily be translated in a different order – "The Word was in the beginning" – proving that "word" is the *subject*.

8. Χριστόν. The *accusative* form is the correct choice, because "Christ" is the *direct object* of the sentence. "Christ" is that which is being "learned," not the one who is doing the learning.

9. Χριστός. The *nominative* form is the correct choice, because "Christ" is the *subject* of the sentence. He is the one who is doing the "remaining."

10. οὐρανόν. The *accusative* form is the correct choice, because "heaven" is the *direct object* of the sentence. It is the thing being "made," not the person who is doing the making.

Lesson 2: Other Patterns

In this lesson, we'd like to show you other spelling patterns for case endings. Other than gender, one big reason that Greek uses **different patterns for case endings** is because of **stem spellings**.

This may sound strange at first, until you think about it. English speakers use different suffix spellings – depending on stem spelling – all the time.

Examples of different spelling patterns in English

When we all were toddlers, just learning to speak English, we naturally picked up the "spelling pattern" of how to make singular nouns into plural nouns. We learned by listening to adults. The pattern was very simple: just attach the sound "s" to the end of a stem. We didn't even have to know the alphabet to begin using this pattern.

Singular: boy   Plural: boy**s**
Singular: girl   Plural: girl**s**
Singular: dog   Plural: dog**s**
Singular: cat   Plural: cat**s**

Not bad for a bunch of toddlers who didn't know their ABCs! But soon, we began to struggle. How were we supposed add the "s" sound to stems which *already* had an "s" sound on the end, like *fox*, *box* or *ax*? Our parents demonstrated a different spelling pattern that worked perfectly for those stems: just add an "es" sound to the end of the stem.

Singular: fox   Plural: fox**es**
Singular: box   Plural: box**es**
Singular: ax   Plural: ax**es**

Over time, we instinctively applied the "es" pattern to other problematic stems, too, like those ending in *ch, sh* or *z*: *churches, crashes, spritzes.*

Joyfully, we went around applying our two patterns to all the nouns in the English language, believing we had them all figured out. Sadly, we hit another wall when we dutifully applied our patterns to *man* and arrived (very logically) at the plural form *mans.* Our parents informed us that, mysteriously, the usual patterns did not apply to that stem. Apparently, exceptional patterns had to be learned as well. In these exceptions, the actual *stem* changed spelling, rather than having letters added to the end of it.

Singular: man   Plural: men
Singular: woman   Plural: women
Singular: mouse   Plural: mice
Singular: tooth   Plural: teeth

Greek spelling patterns vary, just like English

Just like English, the Greek language requires different suffix patterns for different types of stems. In English, the necessity for different patterns is usually just "common sense"; there's no way to to create an extra "s" sound on stems which already end in the "s" sound unless you add an "es." Similarly, in Greek, some spelling patterns are "common sense" accommodations that are made in order for the stem to work well with the ending.

However, some spelling patterns in English seem to have no rhyme or reason. Why not say *mans* and *womans*? Why must it be *men* and *women*? Similarly, some Greek spelling patterns seem to have no rhyme or reason. Sometimes the Greek stem itself will change spellings, just as our English stem *man* changes to *men*, and *mouse* changes to *mice*.

Please don't be concerned about having to learn more patterns. We're always going to take it nice and slow. We'll start with the easy, obvious patterns and give you lots of practice with those. By the time you need to learn the exceptions, you'll feel pretty confident about case endings.

New vocabulary

Before we teach you the next pattern, we need to add a few more nouns to your vocabulary. These all happen to be *feminine nouns*. They are listed here in order of frequency (highest first), according to how many times each word appears in the New Testament. **Please memorize them now.** (A tear-out flashcard page is included at the end of this lesson for your convenience).

Feminine Nouns

Greek word	Our Transliteration	Standard Transliteration	Brief Translation
ἁμαρτία	*hah-mar-TEE-ah*	hamartia	sin, moral failure
βασιλεία	*bah-sih-LAY-ah*	basileia	kingdom, sovereignty, rule, authority
καρδία	*kar-DEE-ah*	kardia	heart, inner self, center, mind, will
φωνή	*fō-NAY*	phōnē	sound, voice, noise
ζωή	*zō-AY*	zōē	life
ψυχή	*psoo-CHAY*	psuchē	soul, life, self

Nominative and accusative case forms for feminine singular nouns whose stems end in alpha

To make things nice and easy, we selected only **feminine singular** nouns whose stems end in **alpha** (α) for this set of scripture examples. Again, **please just focus on the words highlighted in gray.** See if you can figure out the case endings pattern for the nominative and accusative cases.

Passages containing "day"

...ἡμέρα ἤρξατο κλίνειν...
day   began   to decline

...**day** began to decline...
Luke 9:12

...οὐκ οἴδατε τὴν ἡμέραν...
neither you do know the   day

...neither do you know the **day**...
Matthew 25:13

Passages containing "heart"

...ἡ γὰρ καρδία σου οὐκ ἔστιν εὐθεῖα...
the indeed heart of you not is right

...your **heart** is not right...
Acts 8:21

...ὁ Κύριος διήνοιξεν τὴν καρδίαν...
the Lord opened the heart

...the Lord opened [her] **heart**...
Acts 16:14

Passage containing "kingdom"

ἐγερθήσεται γὰρ ἔθνος ἐπὶ ἔθνος καὶ βασιλεία ἐπὶ βασιλείαν...
will rise up indeed nation against nation and kingdom against kingdom

Nation will rise against nation, and **kingdom** against **kingdom**...
Matthew 24:7

Do you see the pattern? In the **nominative case**, there is **no case ending** at all. In this respect, these feminine nouns differ from the masculine nouns in Lesson 1. However, in the **accusative case**, the letter **nu** (ν) is added, which is the same case ending used for the masculine nouns in Lesson 1.

Identifying stems and case endings in feminine singular nouns whose stems end in *alpha*

Here are enlargements of your vocabulary words from the prior three passages, in both nominative and accusative case forms. We've written their stems in outlined lettering and their case endings in solid lettering.

ἡμέρα

day
nominative case

ἡμέραν

day
accusative case

καρδία

heart
nominative case

καρδίαν

heart
accusative case

βασιλεία

kingdom
nominative case

βασιλείαν

kingdom
accusative case

Note that the **nominative** forms have **no case ending letters** at all. They are, in essence, just the "bare" stem itself. The **accusative** forms have the case ending letter of **nu** (ν).

Nominative and accusative case forms for feminine singular nouns whose stems end in eta

You've probably noticed that several of the feminine singular nouns you've learned end in **eta** (η). We'll show you some examples from scripture which contain those nouns. See if you can figure out the case endings pattern for the nominative and accusative cases.

Passages containing "*earth*"

...ἐβοήθησεν ἡ γῆ τῇ γυναικί...
helped   the earth the   woman

...the **earth** helped the woman...
Revelation 12:16

...πατάξαι τὴν γῆν ἐν πάσῃ πληγῇ...
to srike   the   earth with every   plague

...to strike the **earth** with every plague...
Revelation 11:6

Passages containing "*voice*"

...φωνὴ ἐκ τῶν οὐρανῶν λέγουσα...
a voice   out   of the   heavens   saying

...a **voice** out of the heavens said...
Matthew 3:17

...οἴδασιν τὴν φωνὴν αὐτοῦ.
they know   the   voice   of him

...they know his **voice**.
John 10:4

Passages containing "*life*"

ἡ γὰρ ψυχὴ πλεῖόν ἐστιν τῆς τροφῆς...
the indeed life   more than   is   the   food

...**life** is more than food...
Luke 12:23

...δοῦναι τὴν ψυχὴν αὐτοῦ...
to give   the   life   of him

...to give his **life**...
Mark 10:45

All right. We're sure you've noticed that, in the **nominative case**, there is **no case ending** at all, while in the **accusative case**, the letter **nu** (ν) is added. For these two cases, feminine singular nouns whose stems end in **eta** behave exactly like those whose stems end in **alpha**.

Identifying stems and case endings in feminine singular nouns whose stems end in eta

Here are enlargements of your vocabulary words from the prior three passages, in both nominative and accusative case forms. We've written their stems in outlined lettering and their case endings in solid lettering.

earth
nominative case

earth
accusative case

voice, sound
nominative case

voice, sound
accusative case

life, soul
nominative case

life, soul
accusative case

Note that the **nominative** forms have **no case ending letters** at all. They are, in essence, just the "bare" stem itself. The **accusative** forms have the case ending letter of **nu** (ν).

Why bother to categorize nouns by whether they end in alpha or eta?

All six examples of the feminine nouns we showed you behave *in exactly the same way* with regard to their nominative and accusative case endings. It doesn't seem to matter that their stems sometimes end in alpha and sometimes in eta.

Why, then, do Greek grammar books tend to "sort" these feminine nouns into two separate categories? The reason is that, in *other* cases like genitive and dative (especially in their plural forms), their patterns *do* differ slightly. The pattern they will follow all depends on that final stem vowel. We haven't taught you plural nouns or those other cases yet, so you won't really see any differences until we get to those particular lessons. Don't worry about them right now.

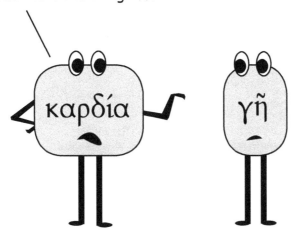

Some Greek nouns just don't get along.

Exercise 2.1 – Riddle Review

Match each English word with its correct Greek spelling, then write its circled "code letter" in the empty circle. The first one is done for you as an example. The circled letters will spell out the answer to the riddle.

Willkommen!

What do they call pastors in Germany?

(S) soul (nominative)   ζωήν ⃝

(E) kingdom (nominative)   βασιλείαν ⃝

(E) voice, sound (accusative)   γῆ (R)

(R) earth (nominative) ⟶   ἁμαρτία ⃝

(H) soul (accusative)   γῆν ⃝

(D) heart (nominative)   καρδίαν ⃝

(A) earth (accusative)

(E) kingdom (accusative)   φωνή ⃝

(N) heart (accusative)   ἡμέραν ⃝

(S) voice, sound (nominative)   βασιλεία ⃝

(G) life (accusative)   ζωή ⃝

(M) sin (nominative)   ψυχήν ⃝

(R) sin (accusative)   φωνήν ⃝

(P) life (nominative)   ἁμαρτίαν ⃝

(H) day (accusative)   καρδία ⃝

                                          ψυχή ⃝

Nominative and accusative case forms for neuter singular nouns whose stems end in omicron

Let's look at another spelling pattern for the nominative and accusative case endings, and this time, let's focus on **neuter** nouns. You learned only two neuter nouns in Book 1: πνεῦμα *pneuma* (spirit, wind, breath) and ὄνομα *onoma* (name, reputation). While they are great nouns to know, they can't be used to illustrate the pattern we need to show you here, because neither has a stem ending in omicron. So, we'll introduce some new Biblical vocabulary that will be useful for illustrating the pattern. We think you'll enjoy learning these powerful New Testament Greek words.

The following words are all **neuter nouns whose stems happen to end in omicron** (o), shown here in order of their frequency of use in the New Testament. **Please memorize them now.**

Neuter Nouns

Greek word	Our Transliteration	Standard Transliteration	Brief Translation
ἔργον	*EHR-gahn*	ergon	work, labor, task, deed, action
τέκνον	*TEK-nahn*	teknon	child, descendant
σημεῖον	*say-MAY-ahn*	sēmeion	sign (typically miraculous, i.e., miracle)
εὐαγγέλιον	*yoo-ahn-GHEL-ee-ahn*	euangelion	good news, the gospel
πρόσωπον	*PRAHSS-ō-pahn*	prosōpon	face, appearance
ἱερόν	*hee-eh-RAHN*	hieron	temple

Unhelpful endings in English

Remember our examples about toddlers learning the plural patterns in English? Those toddlers were able to tell whether most words were plural just by listening to the last sound of the word. If they could hear an "s" sound, they could reasonably guess that the word was plural.

Sadly, those poor kids had no idea what was coming. When it comes to guessing plural versus singular, *no one* is able to win against these words:

> bison
> crossroads
> gallows
> shrimp
> series
> you

Words like these have "unhelpful" endings. All of the words above can be *either* singular or plural number, depending on how they are being used. Yet, some end in "s," and some do not. There's no rhyme or reason to it. The only way to know the number of these words is to pay attention to the *context*.

> That poor baby **bison** is all alone. (singular)
> Those **bison** are trampling my vegetable garden! (plural)
>
> I've been enjoying that new comedy **series**. (singular)
> The network is piloting four new **series** this fall. (plural)
>
> **You** are a wonderful person. (singular)
> **You** are wonderful people. (plural)

Unhelpful endings in Greek

You're about to see an excellent example of an unhelpful ending in Greek: the case ending for the nominative and accusative cases for neuter nouns ending in omicron.

When you see this unhelpful ending, all we ask is that you do not go berserk. Everything is completely under control. We will show you how to use the *context* – just like a Greek toddler would.

Passages containing neuter singular nouns whose stems end in omicron

Compare the case endings of the words highlighted in gray.

Passages containing "*work*"

ἑκάστου τὸ ἔργον φανερὸν γενήσεται...
of each   the   work   manifest   will become

Each man's **work** will become manifest...
1 Corinthians 3:13

...περισσεύητε εἰς πᾶν ἔργον ἀγαθόν.
you might abound   in   every   work   good

...you may abound in every good **work.**
2 Corinthians 9:8

Passages containing "*sign*"

...σημεῖον μέγα ὤφθη ἐν τῷ οὐρανῷ...
a sign   great   was seen in   -   heaven

...a great **sign** appeared in heaven...
Revelation 12:1

...θέλομεν ἀπὸ σοῦ σημεῖον ἰδεῖν.
we wish   from   you   a sign   to see

...we want to see a **sign** from you.
Matthew 12:38

Passages containing "*face*"

...ἔλαμψεν τὸ πρόσωπον αὐτοῦ...
shone   the   face   of him

...his **face** shone...
Matthew 17:2

...τὸ πρόσωπόν σου νίψαι...
the   face   of you   wash

...wash your **face**...
Matthew 6:17

Notice that the **first** scripture in each example demonstrates the **nominative** case, and the **second** demonstrates the **accusative** case, even though **both forms are spelled identically.** The *same* case ending letter, **nu** (ν), is used in *both* the nominative and accusative cases for these types of neuter nouns.

The good news is that the case ending of nu at least narrows it down to two choices out of the five possible cases: *nominative* or *accusative*. From there, you'll use the *context* to determine which of the two it is. Use the "question tests" we taught you in Lesson 1 to figure out the word's grammatical role. If it's a *subject,* then it's nominative. If it's a *direct object,* then it's accusative.

Paradigms – handy charts to make reviewing easier

This lesson is drawing to a close. It's a good time to review all the case ending patterns we learned in lessons 1 and 2.

- For masculine singular nouns whose stems end in omicron (o), the nominative case ending is sigma (ς) and the accusative case ending is nu (ν).

- For feminine singular nouns whose stems end in alpha (α) or eta (η), there is no nominative case ending, and the accusative case ending is nu (ν).

- For neuter singular nouns whose stems end in omicron (o), the nominative case ending is nu (ν) and the accusative case ending is also nu (ν).

Whew! That's a wordy way to review the patterns. Would you like to know a better way?

Most textbooks like to list their patterns in easy, visual chart layouts. Linguists call these charts **paradigms**. The word *paradigm* is an English word having Greek ancestry. The original roots of the word *paradigm* actually mean "side-by-side showing."

Below is a "side-by-side showing" (i.e., a *paradigm*) of all the case endings you have learned so far.

Paradigm of Noun Case Endings... so far*

A dash (-) means that no case ending is used.

	masculine singular whose stems end in omicron (o)	feminine singular whose stems end in alpha or eta (α , η)	neuter singular whose stems end in omicron (o)
nominative case	ς	–	ν
accusative case	ν	ν	ν

*We'll be adding more cases and different spelling patterns to this paradigm eventually.

Textbooks also like to give their students helpful paradigms using actual Greek nouns as examples of how the case endings create all their different forms. Here's one we made up for you. We just grabbed four random nouns from the past lessons that met the requirements of each column and stuck them into the chart from the preceding page. Notice that we expanded the feminine singular column to show *two* example words, one for the stem whose ending vowel is alpha, and the other whose ending vowel is eta.

Paradigm of Noun Case Form Examples

	masculine singular *whose stems end in omicron (o)*	feminine singular *whose stems end in alpha or eta* *(α)*	*(η)*	neuter singular *whose stems end in omicron (o)*
nominative case	λόγος	καρδία	φωνή	ἔργον
accusative case	λόγον	καρδίαν	φωνήν	ἔργον

You can create your own example paradigms just like we did in the one above. Exercise 2.2 on the next page will give you a chance to do that.

paradox

paradise

parapets

paradigms

Exercise 2.2 – Paradigm Showtime!

Think you know your stuff? It's time to *show* it with your first **Paradigm Showtime!** Using the words in the word bank, fill in the paradigm with the correct case forms for each word. Then, write the translation of each word underneath the paradigm. **Hint:** The words in the bank are **not in any particular order, so pay attention to their genders and stem spellings.** You can refer to Lessons 1 and 2 to refresh your memory.

	masculine singular *whose stems end in omicron (o)*	feminine singular *whose stems end in alpha or eta* (α) (η)	neuter singular *whose stems end in omicron (o)*
nominative case			
accusative case			

Translation: _____ _____ _____ _____

WORD BANK

τέκνον   ἀδελφός   ψυχή   ἡμέρα

ANSWER KEY

ἀδελφός	ἡμέρα	ψυχή	τέκνον
ἀδελφόν	ἡμέραν	ψυχήν	τέκνον
"brother"	"day"	"soul, life"	"child, descendant"

Lesson 2 Flashcards

Carefully tear out this page and cut along the lines to create a set of flashcards.

ἁμαρτία	βασιλεία
καρδία	φωνή
ζωή	ψυχή
ἔργον	τέκνον

We restricted ourselves to **partial** definitions on the cards, to make memorization easier for you. But remember: These are not the *only* meanings. The true meanings of these words as they are used throughout the New Testament are much more expansive. Whenever you learn a new Greek vocabulary word, make a strong mental effort *not* to restrict yourself to a single, mechanical definition. Word meanings are *always* flexible within the context of any living, fluid language.

bah-sih-LAY-ah kingdom, rule noun, feminine, singular, nominative (This word was introduced in Book 2, Lesson 2)	*hah-mar-TEE-ah* sin, moral failure noun, feminine, singular, nominative (This word was introduced in Book 2, Lesson 2)
fō-NAY voice, sound noun, feminine, singular, nominative (This word was introduced in Book 2, Lesson 2)	*kar-DEE-ah* heart, inner self noun, feminine, singular, nominative (This word was introduced in Book 2, Lesson 2)
psoo-CHAY soul, self, life noun, feminine, singular, nominative (This word was introduced in Book 2, Lesson 2)	*zō-AY* life noun, feminine, singular, nominative (This word was introduced in Book 2, Lesson 2)
TEK-nahn child, descendant noun, neuter, singular, nominative (This word was introduced in Book 2, Lesson 2)	*EHR-gahn* work, deed, action noun, neuter, singular, nominative (This word was introduced in Book 2, Lesson 2)

σημεῖον	εὐαγγέλιον
πρόσωπον	ἱερόν

yoo-ahn-GHEL-ee-ahn good news, gospel noun, neuter, singular, nominative (This word was introduced in Book 2, Lesson 2)	*say-MAY-ahn* sign, miracle noun, neuter, singular, nominative (This word was introduced in Book 2, Lesson 2)
hee-eh-RAHN temple noun, neuter, singular, nominative (This word was introduced in Book 2, Lesson 2)	*PRAHSS-ō-pahn* face, appearance noun, neuter, singular, nominative (This word was introduced in Book 2, Lesson 2)

Lesson 3: Genitive and Dative

When you first begin to tackle some of the grammar that goes along with Greek, it can be easy to get discouraged or lost among the details. Many students begin to wonder, *What's the point of knowing all this? Is it all really necessary?*

If you want to understand the intent of God's scriptures for yourself without relying on someone else to translate it for you, the answer is "yes." Understanding "grammar stuff" like noun cases, for example, is sometimes the *only* key to getting at a sentence's true meaning in scripture.

Let us share just one insight that can come from understanding cases. After you read this, you'll feel truly inspired to keep going with your Greek studies.

Peace on earth, good will toward *everyone?*

When the shepherds heard the angels saying the words of Luke 2:14 outside of Bethlehem on that wonderful night, what *exactly* did they hear? Let's compare some popular English translations to find out. We've included the abbreviation of each translation and the year it was written. All the translations begin with the same essential meaning – "Glory to God in the highest" – but they end with some very *different* phrases:

KJV (1611) ... and on earth peace, good will toward men.*

WBT (1833) ... and on earth peace, good will towards men.

YLT (1862) ... and upon earth peace, among men -- good will.

DRB (1752) ... and on earth peace to men of good will.

NIV (1978) ... and on earth peace to those on whom his favor rests.

NAS (1971) ... And on earth peace among men with whom He is pleased.

CSB (2004) ... and peace on earth to people he favors!

ISV (2011) ... and peace on earth to people who enjoy his favor!

GWT (1995) ... and on earth peace to those who have his good will!

*The New King James, written in 1982, includes a footnote with an alternate translation: "and on earth peace, toward men of good will."

The first set of scriptures seem to be saying that the peace and good will are toward *all humanity*. The middle scripture seems to say that the peace is toward *men of good will*. The third set of scriptures seem to say that the peace is toward *those who enjoy God's good will (favor)*. Well, which is it? And why all the differences?

Before we answer... did you notice a pattern in the years in which the translations were written? All the translations in the top set (as well as the middle one), were written more than a hundred years ago. All those in the bottom set were written relatively recently. So, here's the answer. The translators of the top set were looking at Greek manuscripts that contain the word εὐδοκία, meaning *good will* or *favor* in the **nominative** case. The translators of the bottom set were looking at much older Greek manuscripts that contain a slightly different spelling of the same word. In the older Greek manuscripts, it is spelled εὐδοκίας, meaning *good will* or *favor* in the **genitive** case. Even though we haven't yet taught you about the genitive case and what it represents, we hope that you noticed the extra sigma on the end of the word here, which indicates a different case ending.

All the translations did an excellent job with whatever Greek manuscripts they had available at the time, but the case ending of sigma made a *huge* difference in their results.

Because they were translating the word from the nominative case, the top set of translations reflects a desire on God's part to pour out his peace and favor upon *all* mankind with His saving grace. This great desire of God is certainly an undeniable fact, but "good will toward all humanity" presents almost a "generic" application of His grace, or perhaps a "partial" truth. It only presents half the picture of how His peace and salvation truly work.

God offers His salvation freely to *everyone*, indeed. And thank God for that! In *that* sense, His peace and favor really are extended toward all humanity. But the Bible teaches again and again that God's peace only *remains* upon those who *receive* His grace by faith in Jesus. Those who reject salvation (and, sadly, that's the majority of humankind) can never be in any position to receive and enjoy God's eternal favor and peace. "There is no peace, says the LORD, for the wicked" (Isaiah 48:22, cf. 57:21). And it was Jesus Himself who said, "Do not think that I have come to bring peace to the earth. I have not come to bring peace, but a sword" (Matthew 10:34).

Due to their awareness of that final sigma in the older Greek manuscripts of Luke 2:14, modern translators are not *allowed* to express God's peace and favor as a generic application to all humanity – not even if they really want to! They find themselves *restricted* to the *exact* meaning of the sentence, which is established by the Greek grammar itself. In Luke 2:14, the genitive case of the noun makes it compulsory to apply God's favor specifically, not generically. In other words, the Greek grammar of Luke 2:14 *limits* God's peace and favor to *certain people*.

Based on the vast commentary of scripture as a whole, it is self-evident that this specific group of people who obtain peace and favor from God are those who have a *saving faith in Messiah Jesus*. This understanding of verse 14 also better fits the context of the whole passage. Remember: the angel introduces Jesus with the terms *Savior, Messiah* and *Lord* in verse 11, clearly stating the exact prerequisites of how Jesus must be perceived (and received) by those who expect to obtain God's favor and peace.

The bottom line? That single letter – sigma – changes the noun's case, which alters the whole thrust of the verse's meaning. **This is why it is crucial to understand Greek grammar.**

Defining the genitive case

Now that you're all charged up and inspired to tackle the genitive and dative cases, let's begin with the genitive. You'll enjoy this case; it's fairly straightforward.

The **genitive** case in Greek is most often used when a noun is showing **possession**. You can think of this as "ownership" if you like, but a more generic way to discover nouns in the genitive case is by using the "of" test. If you can put "of" in front of a noun, it is in the genitive case. Another test that sometimes works is to add an apostrophe to the noun, which also indicates possession. Let's look at some English examples; we've underlined any words which would be in the **genitive** case if they had been written in Greek.

> the law of **God**   *or*   **God**'s law
>
> the writings of **Paul**   *or*   **Paul**'s writings
>
> the city of **David**   *or*   **David**'s city

It probably occurred to you, however, that the "city of David" was *named* after David and *relates* to David in many ways, but he didn't actually *own* the entire city. Therefore, the genitive case is not always about *literal* ownership. Sometimes, the genitive case is *figurative* and can mean "belonging with" or "pertaining to." If you run across figurative uses of this case in your Greek studies, it's no problem! You can still use the "of" test to discover if the word is in the genitive case. Here are some figurative examples of the Greek genitive case (shown here in English, for your convenience). Notice how clearly this case is revealed by using the "of" test.

> body of **sin**   *i.e., "sinful body," Romans 6:6*
>
> the poor of **the saints**   *Romans 15:26*
>
> sign of **circumcision**   *Romans 4:11*
>
> day of **salvation**   *2 Corinthians 6:2*

Technically, you can even apply the apostrophe test to the above phrases, although some of the results might sound slightly awkward in English: *sin's body, the saints' poor, circumcision's sign, salvation's day.* We personally prefer the "of" test, but please use whichever test you like best.

Genitive case forms for masculine singular nouns whose stems end in omicron

Here are examples from scripture of the genitive case for masculine nouns whose stems end in omicron. Look for the case ending letter on each genitive noun, which is highlighted in gray.

Passages containing "world"

...τὰς βασιλείας τοῦ κόσμου...   ...the kingdoms of the **world**... *Matthew 4:8*

...τὴν ἁμαρτίαν τοῦ κόσμου.   ...the sin of the **world**. *John 1:29*

...ἐγὼ οὐκ εἰμὶ ἐκ τοῦ κόσμου.   ...I am not of the **world**. *John 17:14*

Passages containing "word"

...ὑπηρέται γενόμενοι τοῦ λόγου.   ...servants of the **word**. *Luke 1:2*

...ὑπεροχὴν λόγου...   ...excellency of **speech**. *1 Corinthians 2:1*

...γίνεσθε δὲ ποιηταὶ λόγου...   ...be doers of the **word**. *James 1:22*

Passages containing "God"

...πνεῦμα θεοῦ...   ...spirit of **God**... *Matthew 3:16*

...υἱοὶ θεοῦ...   ...sons of **God**... *Matthew 5:9*

...ἡ βασιλεία τοῦ θεοῦ....   ...the kingdom of **God**... *Matthew 12:28*

You will have noticed that **the genitive case ending** in these instances **is the letter upsilon**, υ.*

*Technically, the *actual* case ending is an omicron. However, as soon as it gets added alongside the omicron that is already at the end of the stem, the added omicron *changes* to an upsilon. The suffix *contracts* from οο to ου. Don't worry about this little spelling rule, though. It's okay to just think of the genitive case ending as "adding an upsilon."

Genitive case forms for feminine singular nouns whose stems end in alpha or eta

Look for the case ending letter on each genitive noun, which is highlighted in gray. This time, we'll only show three examples for each type of stem; we think you get the idea.

Stems ending in alpha

...τῇ πωρώσει τῆς καρδίας..   ...the hardness of the **heart**... *Mark 3:5*

...ἦλθον ἡμέρας ὁδὸν...   ...they went a **day's** journey... *Luke 2:44*

...δοῦλός ἐστιν τῆς ἁμαρτίας.   ...is a slave of **sin**. *John 8:34*

Stems ending in eta

...ἀποβολὴ γὰρ ψυχῆς...   ...loss of **life**... *Acts 27:22*

...ὁ ἄρτος τῆς ζωῆς...   ...the bread of **life**... *John 6:35*

...τὸ ἅλας τῆς γῆς...   ...the salt of the **earth**. *Matthew 5:13*

You will have noticed that **the case ending** on each genitive noun in these instances is the letter **sigma**, ς. At first, this might seem confusing, because you've already seen sigma used as a case ending in another situation, right? You know that sigma is used for the *nominative* case ending for masculine nouns ending in omicron. Now, here's that same letter being used on *feminine* nouns to indicate the *genitive* case! Well, no worries. There's an easy way to keep them straight.

Notice that all the nouns in the examples above end in either alpha-sigma (ας) or eta-sigma (ης). This indicates that their *stems* end in alpha or eta. Notice that *none* of the above examples end in omicron-sigma (ος). If they did, it would mean that their *stems* end in omicron (and, yes, in *that* situation, you would indeed have a masculine singular nominative noun).

We suggest that you begin a new habit: scan the *entire* last syllable of a word rather than just the final letter. It's the best way to tell the difference between many similar-looking situations.

A reminder: The accent marks on some of the nouns do change under different conditions. You may ignore any accent changes for now. They don't affect the things we're learning about.

Genitive case forms for neuter singular nouns whose stems end in omicron

Look for the case ending letter on each genitive noun, which is highlighted in gray.

...ποιητὴς ἔργου...   ...a doer of the **work**... *James 1:25*

...τὸ πτερύγιον τοῦ ἱεροῦ.   ...the pinnacle of the **temple**. *Matthew 4:5*

...τὸ εἶδος τοῦ προσώπου...   ...the appearance of the **face**... *Luke 9:29*

You will have noticed that **the case ending** on each genitive noun in these instances **is the letter upsilon**, υ (just like for masculine singular nouns whose stems end in omicron).*

*Again, the *actual* case ending that gets added is an omicron. Just like the earlier situation, the suffix has to contract from οο to ου. It's okay to think of it as just "adding an upsilon."

Feeling hazy? Good! You're completely normal!

Are you beginning to feel hazy about all these patterns? Are you having a great deal of trouble keeping them straight? That's *normal*. Unless you grew up speaking Greek, you're *never* going to remember them all. If you find it difficult to remember case endings, you're in very good company.

Many Bible scholars who have spent their *entire adult lives* studying Greek still can't remember many of the case endings. We, the authors of this book, certainly can't. Like all native English speakers, we have to rely on a combination of paradigm charts and the context of the passage just to figure out what a Greek word's grammatical role is.

So, *please* don't feel bad about getting confused or forgetting the case endings. That's the whole reason paradigm charts were invented. Use them as often as you need or want.

Don't forget the end goal. It's *not* to memorize Greek case endings. The goal is to love God with our lives, deeds, attitudes and thoughts. It's to immerse ourselves in His word and let Him work His miracles within us. Soak up whatever you can from this workbook, enjoy the ride, and don't sweat the small stuff.

Adding the genitive case to our paradigm

Speaking of having to refer to paradigms a lot... how about we stop right now and add the genitive case to our paradigm from the last lesson? This is a great time to slow down, take a deep breath, and review what we've learned.

Paradigm of Noun Case Endings... so far

	masculine singular *whose stems end in omicron (o)*	feminine singular *whose stems end in alpha or eta (α , η)*	neuter singular *whose stems end in omicron (o)*
nominative case	ς	–	ν
genitive case	υ	ς	υ
accusative case	ν	ν	ν

Notice that we inserted the genitive row *in between* the nominative and accusative rows, rather than adding it to the bottom of the chart. (All modern paradigms list the cases in a standard order, so, for the sake of consistency, we will follow that standard order in our paradigms, too.)

Now, take a look at the paradigm which uses actual nouns as examples. We inserted a row for the genitive case there, too.

Paradigm of Noun Case Form Examples

	masculine singular *whose stems end in omicron (o)*	feminine singular *whose stems end in alpha or eta* (α)　　　　　(η)		neuter singular *whose stems end in omicron (o)*
nominative case	λόγος	καρδία	φωνή	ἔργον
genitive case	λόγου	καρδίας	φωνῆς	ἔργου
accusative case	λόγον	καρδίαν	φωνήν	ἔργον

It's nice to be able to look at entire words in the paradigm, isn't it? Being able to see the stem letters really clears up any confusion about endings that share the same case ending letter.

Exercise 3.1 – Riddle Review

For each scripture phrase, **match the underlined word with its Greek translation.** Be careful to select the correct case form. Then write its circled "code letter" in the empty circle to solve the riddle.

Who was the shortest person in the Bible?

(A) ...love not the **world**...   κόσμος ◯

(I) ...be doers of the **word**...   φωνή ◯

(H) ...I speak to those who know the **law**...

(H) ...love is the fulfillment of the **law**...   ἁμαρτίας ◯

(H) ...**God** is spirit...   καρδίας ◯

(D) ...spirit of **God**...   κόσμου (S)

(T) ...I am the bread of **life**...   γῆ ◯

(L) ...the Lord opened her **heart**...   λόγου ◯

(B) ...the **earth** helped the woman...   καρδίαν ◯

(S) ...who takes away the sin of the **world**...   ζωή ◯

(T) ...the **voice** of one crying in the wilderness...   κόσμον ◯

(E) ...you shall love the Lord your **God**...   θεοῦ ◯

(D) ...I am the resurrection and the **life**...   ζωῆς ◯

(S) ...**sin** entered the world...   θεός ◯

(I) ...you are the salt of the **earth**...   βασιλείαν ◯

(E) ...seek first the **kingdom**...

(T) ...proclaiming the gospel of the **kingdom**...   ἁμαρτία ◯

(I) ...the **world** is passing away...   νόμον ◯

(W) ...a slave of **sin**...   γῆν ◯

(U) ...to strike the **earth** with every plague...   νόμου ◯

(A) ...the hardness of the **heart**...   γῆς ◯

                                                           βασιλείας ◯

                                                            θεόν ◯

Answer: It was Bildad the Shuhite.

Defining the dative case

The **dative** case is close to the English concept of the **indirect object.** The **dative** case in Greek actually has **more expansive usages** than just that, so you can *usually* test for it by placing the test words *to, in* or *with* in front of the noun. If you suspect there's an indirect object in your sentence, you can ask the test question, "to whom" (or "for whom") is the action being done?

Before we talk about all the uses of the dative case, we need to first define what an indirect object is, since it is one of the uses. Let's start with easy examples of the indirect object in English.

The indirect object in English

Here's one of our simple English sentences from Lesson 1.

The man threw a ball.

Recall that the *man* is the *subject*. He's the one *doing* the action. The *ball* is the *direct object*. It's the thing *directly receiving* the action. It's the thing *directly being acted on.*

An *indirect object* is something or someone who is *indirectly affected by the activity*. It is *somehow* involved in the action, but not *directly* involved. Let's add an indirect object to our simple sentence. We've underlined it here.

The man threw a ball to the **dog**.

Ask the question, "To whom, or for whom, was the ball being thrown?" Answer: the dog. Here are some other examples of the indirect object in English (underlined for your convenience).

Angela cooked dinner for **Joel**.	Subject: "Who is cooking?" *Angela* Direct object: "What's being cooked?" *dinner* Indirect object: "For whom?" *Joel*
Angela cooked **him** dinner.	Subject: "Who is cooking?" *Angela* Direct object: "What's being cooked?" *dinner* Indirect object: "For whom?" *him*
I teach the **students** Greek.	Subject: "Who is teaching?" *I* Direct object: "What's being taught?" *Greek* Indirect object: "To whom?" *the students*
He tells **them** the truth.	Subject: "Who is telling?" *He* Direct object: "What's being told?" *the truth* Indirect object: "To whom?" *them*

When the Greek dative case acts as an indirect object

Let's look at some scriptures in which the dative case noun is acting as an indirect object.

...ἀναστήσει σπέρμα τῷ ἀδελφῷ...   ...will raise up seed for the **brother**... *Mt. 22:24*

..ζωὴν διδοὺς τῷ κόσμῳ.   ...giving life to the **world**. *Jn. 6:33*

The versatile applications of the dative case

As we mentioned earlier, the Greek dative case actually has a wider range of applications than just the indirect object.   It can also speak of the *means*, or *agency*, by which an action is done. A question test for this might be "How?" or "By what means?" Sometimes it speaks of the *location* in which an action occurs. "Where?" would be the question. This is the reason the test words of *to, in* or *with* may be used to determine if a noun is in the dative case.

Here are examples of *means* or *agency*. The test words *in* or *with* fit these examples. The question tests *How?* or *By what means?* work well with these.

...ἐξέβαλεν τὰ πνεύματα λόγῳ...   He cast out the spirits with a **word**... *Mt. 8:16*

...ἵνα αὐτὸν ἀγρεύσωσιν λόγῳ.   ...that they might catch Him in **speech**... *Mk. 12:13*

Here are examples of *location*. The test word *in* works here, but in some situations you might also use the word *at*. For these, the question test *Where?* applies.

...ἐν τῇ καρδίᾳ τῆς γῆς...   ... in the **heart** of the earth... *Mt. 12:40*

...ἐν τῷ ἱερῷ...   ...in the **temple**... *Mt. 21:15*

The dative case has many other applications, too. It would be difficult to enumerate them all. They include, but aren't limited to:

advantage / disadvantage (test word *against*), "you testify against **yourselves**"
reference / respect (test words *regarding, concerning, about*), "regarding the **Son** of Man"
sphere (test words *in/with reference to, regarding*), "in regard to **wickedness**"
feeling/ethical (test words *for me, as far as I'm concerned*), "for **me**, to live is Christ"
destination (test words *to, toward*), "he walked toward the **house**"
recipient (test word *to*), "from Paul, to the **saints**"
manner (test words *in, with*), "he speaks in **public**," "proclaim Christ with **sincerity**"
measure (test word *by*), "by **much more** we are saved"
cause (test words *due to, because of*), "due to **unbelief**," "because of these **bonds**"

Other applications include *time*, *material*, and *content*. Even some direct objects, or nouns/ pronouns which follow certain prepositions or adjectives, can take on the dative case.

Short and long vowels

Before we go into the case endings for the dative case, we need to describe the difference between a *long* and *short* vowel in Greek. All the Greek vowels have long and short versions of themselves.

The terms *long* and *short* mean different things for Greek vowels than they do for English vowels. In ancient Greek, at the very least, *long* meant you spent "twice as long" (time-wise) saying the vowel (although few modern people observe this). A *long* vowel, then, was "elongated" in time. In addition to this time lengthening, certain vowels' long versions came to have a completely different vowel sound than their short versions. For example, iota, which was ordinarily pronounced "ih," came to be pronounced "ee" in the long version.

Up until now, it hasn't been crucial for you to know that long and short vowels even exist. Just by pronouncing different Greek words using the cheat sheet we gave you in Book 1, you've *already* been using the long and short versions of the vowels without even knowing it. Now that you're about to learn the dative case endings, though, you've come to the place where you need to know some of this terminology.

Three Greek vowels **always keep the same forms (i.e., letter representations)**, whether they are being pronounced in their "short" or "long" versions:

short		**long**		
α	"ah"	α	"aah"	(same as short sound, but elongated in time)
ι	"ih"	ι	"ee"	(a different sound, also elongated in time)
υ	"oo"	υ	"ooh"	(same as short sound, but elongated in time)

In other words, alpha *always* looks like an alpha, whether you are being asked to pronounce it long or short.

However, the other four vowels are actually **short and long versions of one another.** The eta is the long version of the epsilon. And the omega is the long version of the omicron. The difference with these four vowels is that the ancient Greeks decided for some reason to create unique letter shapes to differentiate between their short and long sounds, rather than just having the same letter shape for both sounds.

short		**long**		
ε	"eh"	η	"ay"	(a different sound, also elongated in time)
ο	"ah"	ω	"ōh"	(a different sound, also elongated in time)

By the way, if you are ever asked to "**lengthen**" a Greek vowel, that just means you need to **convert the vowel to its long version.** For example, if you happen to start out with an alpha (α) and the grammar requires you to lengthen it, it will remain looking like an α. But if you start out with an epsilon (ε) and you are asked to lengthen it, you'll end up changing it into an eta (η).

The case ending for the dative case

This time, rather than asking you to figure out the pattern for the dative case all by yourself, we're going to describe it to you, because it's more disguised than the other case endings.

For the types of singular nouns we've been studying, the **rule for the dative case ending** is this: **(1)** *lengthen* **the final stem vowel, and (2) add an** *iota subscript* **underneath that vowel.** "Lengthen," as we said earlier, simply means, "Change the short version of the vowel to its long version." "Iota subscript" means "that tiny iota written underneath the vowel." *

It would help to see some examples. Here is a list of **masculine singular nouns with stems that end in omicron.** The left column shows them as we first taught them to you – in the nice, familiar, nominative case. We highlighted the final stem vowel in gray. The right column shows them in the dative case, with the two required changes made.

nominative	dative
θεός	θεῷ
Χριστός	Χριστῷ
υἱός	υἱῷ
ἀδελφός	ἀδελφῷ
λόγος	λόγῳ
οὐρανός	οὐρανῷ
νόμος	νόμῳ
κόσμος	κόσμῳ

Notice what needed to be done to create the dative case. Ignore that final sigma case ending on the nominative form just for a moment. Just mentally strip it off and focus only on the *stem* of the word. In **step 1**, the final stem vowel (omicron) was *lengthened* (converted into omega). In **step 2**, the *iota subscript* was added underneath it. Not too hard, right?

By the way, you might have noticed that some of these words **changed accent marks** from acute to circumflex. Not only does *this* happen on occasion, but sometimes accent marks **shift positions,** jumping from one syllable to another (although that didn't occur in the examples above). Don't be alarmed if you see shifting accents later on in your studies. While shifting accents will force you to emphasize a different syllable during pronunciation, they'll have no effect on which case endings are attached, nor on the grammatical functions of the case forms. Those attributes are independent of any accent mark changes.

---

*Remember in Book 1 how we told you that the iota subscript isn't pronounced out loud, but there would be times you'd have to be able to recognize it for grammar reasons? This is one of those times.

How about our **feminine singular nouns with stems that end in alpha or eta?** The same two-part rule applies. The only thing is, when you go to lengthen the alpha, it's still going to look like an alpha, because the long version and short version of that vowel look identical. And, when you go to lengthen the eta, you'll realize that it already *is* a long version vowel! So, that's going to stay the same, too. Since you aren't really changing the appearance of either of these final stem vowels, the only thing left for you to do is add the iota subscript.

nominative	dative
ἡμέρα	ἡμέρᾳ
καρδία	καρδίᾳ
βασιλεία	βασιλείᾳ
ἁμαρτία	ἁμαρτίᾳ
γῆ	γῇ
φωνή	φωνῇ
ζωή	ζωῇ
ψυχή	ψυχῇ

Last but not least are the **neuter singular nouns with stems that end in omicron.** Adding the dative case ending is the same process as it was for the masculine singular nouns on the previous page. Again, just mentally strip off the nominative case ending of nu (ν) to reveal the stem. Change the final stem vowel (omicron) into its long form (omega), and add the iota subscript.

nominative	dative
ἔργον	ἔργῳ
τέκνον	τέκνῳ
πρόσωπον	προσώπῳ
ἱερόν	ἱερῷ

Adding the dative case to our paradigms

Let's add the dative case to our two paradigms. For ease of reading, the iota is always typeset as a full-size iota in the case endings paradigm, even though in actual Greek words it is written as a subscript.

Paradigm of Noun Case Endings... so far

	masculine singular *whose stems end in omicron (ο)*	feminine singular *whose stems end in alpha or eta (α , η)*	neuter singular *whose stems end in omicron (ο)*
nominative case	ς	–	ν
genitive case	υ	ς	υ
dative case*	ι*	ι*	ι*
accusative case	ν	ν	ν

*For singular nouns whose stems fit the descriptions above, the iota will always be an iota *subscript* for the dative case, and the stem's final vowel will always be *lengthened* before placing that iota subscript underneath it.

Paradigm of Noun Case Form Examples

	masculine singular *whose stems end in omicron (ο)*	feminine singular *whose stems end in alpha or eta* (α) (η)	neuter singular *whose stems end in omicron (ο)*
nominative case	λόγος	καρδία φωνή	ἔργον
genitive case	λόγου	καρδίας φωνῆς	ἔργου
dative case	λόγῳ	καρδίᾳ φωνῇ	ἔργῳ
accusative case	λόγον	καρδίαν φωνήν	ἔργον

We thought it would also be convenient for you to have a list of the four case forms for the types of nouns you've studied so far. In the column headers, the abbreviation "sg." means "singular." (Remember, we've learned only the singular forms of our nouns so far. We'll learn plurals soon.)

	nom. sg.	gen. sg.	dat. sg.	acc. sg.	meaning
masculine nouns stems ending in omicron	θεός	θεοῦ	θεῷ	θεόν	God, god
	κύριος	κυρίου	κυρίῳ	κύριον	Lord, lord, master
	ἄνθρωπος	ἀνθρώπου	ἀνθρώπῳ	ἄνθρωπον	man, humankind
	Χριστός	Χριστοῦ	Χριστῷ	Χριστόν	Christ, anointed one
	υἱός	υἱοῦ	υἱῷ	υἱόν	son, descendant
	ἀδελφός	ἀδελφοῦ	ἀδελφῷ	ἀδελφόν	brother
	λόγος	λόγου	λόγῳ	λόγον	word, statement
	οὐρανός	οὐρανοῦ	οὐρανῷ	οὐρανόν	heaven, sky
	νόμος	νόμου	νόμῳ	νόμον	law, principle
	κόσμος	κόσμου	κόσμῳ	κόσμον	world, universe
feminine nouns stems ending in alpha	ἡμέρα	ἡμέρας	ἡμέρᾳ	ἡμέραν	day
	καρδία	καρδίας	καρδίᾳ	καρδίαν	heart, inner self
	βασιλεία	βασιλείας	βασιλείᾳ	βασιλείαν	kingdom, sovereignty
	ἁμαρτία	ἁμαρτίας	ἁμαρτίᾳ	ἁμαρτίαν	sin, moral failure
feminine nouns stems ending in eta	γῆ	γῆς	γῇ	γῆν	earth, land
	φωνή	φωνῆς	φωνῇ	φωνήν	sound, voice, noise
	ζωή	ζωῆς	ζωῇ	ζωήν	life
	ψυχή	ψυχῆς	ψυχῇ	ψυχήν	soul, breath, life
neuter nouns stems ending in omicron	ἔργον	ἔργου	ἔργῳ	ἔργον	work, deed, act
	τέκνον	τέκνου	τέκνῳ	τέκνον	child, descendant
	σημεῖον	σημείου	σημείῳ	σημεῖον	sign, miracle
	εὐαγγέλιον	εὐαγγελίου	εὐαγγελίῳ	εὐαγγέλιον	good news, gospel
	πρόσωπον	προσώπου	προσώπῳ	πρόσωπον	face, appearance
	ἱερόν	ἱεροῦ	ἱερῷ	ἱερόν	temple

Exercise 3.2 – Paradigm Showtime!

Using the words in the word bank, **fill in the paradigm with the correct case forms for each word.** Feel free to refer to the charts on the previous pages for the correct spellings.

	masculine singular *whose stems end in omicron (o)*	feminine singular *whose stems end in alpha or eta* *(α) (η)*	neuter singular *whose stems end in omicron (o)*
nominative case			
genitive case			
dative case			
accusative case			

Translation: _____ _____ _____

WORD BANK

βασιλεία   φωνή   ἔργον   οὐρανός

ANSWER KEY

οὐρανός	βασιλεία	φωνή	ἔργον
οὐρανοῦ	βασιλείας	φωνῆς	ἔργου
οὐρανῷ	βασιλείᾳ	φωνῇ	ἔργῳ
οὐρανόν	βασιλείαν	φωνήν	ἔργον
"heaven, sky"	"kingdom"	"voice, sound"	"work, deed"

Exercise 3.3 – Hidden Picture

In this puzzle, **each row contains the answer or answers to the question at its left.** For each English definition at the left of each row, **find its matching Greek translation,** *but only in that particular row.* **Then shade the answer in with your pencil.** Once you've finished shading your answers, the shaded boxes will create a picture. Be careful to **find the spellings with the correct case endings**; some of the choices are pretty tricky. Also, sometimes the words switch order; the second word may appear first in the grid (we did one of those, row 5, as an example). The case abbreviations are: N-nominative, G-genitive, D-dative, A-accusative. Don't hesitate to refer to your paradigms or word lists if you need them. The answer key to this puzzle is on the back.

ROW:

α	β	δ	γ	ῆ	ε	ρ	σ	ξ	γ	ῆ	υ	ι	ο	ν	δ	η	α	π	τ
υ	ς	φ	ω	ν	ή	ω	ε	φ	ω	ν	ῆ	β	θ	φ	ω	ν	ῆ	ς	μ
κ	ό	σ	μ	ο	ῳ	α	κ	ό	σ	μ	ο	υ	δ	κ	ό	σ	μ	ο	ν
π	ρ	ό	σ	ω	β	π	ρ	ο	σ	ώ	π	ο	υ	ν	ω	π	ι	χ	ω
ἔ	ρ	γ	ο	ν	ἱ	ε	ρ	ῷ	ν	π	ἔ	ρ	γ	ῳ	ἱ	ε	ρ	ό	ν
θ	ε	ο	ῦ	λ	ό	γ	ο	υ	ς	ο	ἱ	ε	ρ	ό	ν	θ	ε	ο	ς
α	δ	ε	δ	ἀ	δ	ε	λ	φ	ό	ν	κ	ό	σ	μ	ῳ	κ	ο	σ	μ
γ	ῆ	α	ι	ε	ὐ	α	γ	γ	έ	λ	ι	ο	ν	γ	ῆ	π	ρ	ο	σ
τ	ε	κ	τ	τ	έ	κ	ν	ῳ	ο	υ	ή	μ	έ	ρ	α	μ	ε	ρ	α
ψ	υ	χ	ῆ	ψ	υ	χ	ῆ	ς	ψ	υ	ν	ό	μ	ο	ς	ν	ό	μ	υ
λ	ο	γ	ο	ῆ	μ	έ	ρ	α	ο	ι	λ	ό	γ	ο	ν	μ	ε	ρ	ψ
ι	ε	ρ	ο	ν	ό	μ	ο	ν	ο	μ	ἱ	ε	ρ	ο	ῦ	ρ	ω	ρ	σ
π	ρ	ο	θ	γ	ῆ	ζ	ω	ή	α	ι	ἔ	ρ	γ	ο	ν	ε	ρ	ρ	γ
α	ψ	ο	π	ψ	υ	χ	ῆ	ψ	υ	χ	ή	ν	β	ψ	υ	χ	ῆ	ς	π
λ	υ	π	ρ	θ	ε	ό	ς	β	θ	ε	ό	ν	ε	ο	χ	θ	ε	ο	ῦ
λ	ο	γ	ο	ψ	α	ζ	ω	ή	ν	ζ	ω	ῆ	ς	β	δ	ω	ι	κ	λ
ε	ρ	γ	γ	ο	ἔ	ρ	γ	ῳ	ἔ	ρ	γ	ο	υ	ἔ	ρ	γ	ο	ν	ν
κ	α	ρ	δ	ί	ᾳ	κ	κ	α	ρ	δ	ί	α	λ	α	μ	β	δ	α	α
π	ρ	ο	σ	σ	π	ρ	ο	σ	ώ	π	ῳ	π	ρ	ό	σ	ω	π	ο	ν
β	α	β	α	σ	ι	λ	ε	ί	α	ν	β	α	σ	ι	λ	ε	ί	α	β

Row labels (at left):

1. earth-N
2. voice-D
3. world-G
4. face-G
5. work-D, temple-D
6. word-G, temple-N
7. brother-A, world-D
8. earth-D, gospel-N
9. child-D, day-N
10. law-N, soul-G
11. day-D, word-A
12. law-A, temple-G
13. earth-D, life-N, work-N
14. soul-N
15. God-A
16. life-G
17. deed-G
18. heart-N
19. face-D
20. kingdom-A

Exercise 3.3 – Answer Key

ROW:

1. earth-N	α	β	δ	γ	ῇ	ε	ρ	σ	ξ	γ	ῆ	υ	ι	ο	ν	δ	η	α	π	τ
2. voice-D	υ	ς	φ	ω	ν	ή	ω	ε	φ	ω	ν	ῇ	β	θ	φ	ω	ν	ῆ	ς	μ
3. world-G	κ	ό	σ	μ	ο	ῳ	α	κ	ό	σ	μ	ο	υ	δ	κ	ό	σ	μ	ο	ν
4. face-G	π	ρ	ό	σ	ω	β	π	ρ	ο	σ	ώ	π	ο	υ	ν	ω	π	ι	χ	ω
5. work-D, temple-D	ἔ	ρ	γ	ο	ν	ι	ε	ρ	ῷ	ν	π	ἔ	ρ	γ	ῳ	ι	ε	ρ	ό	ν
6. word-G, temple-N	θ	ε	ο	ῦ	λ	ό	γ	ο	υ	ς	ο	ἱ	ε	ρ	ό	ν	θ	ε	ο	ς
7. brother-A, world-D	α	δ	ε	δ	ἀ	δ	ε	λ	φ	ό	ν	κ	ό	σ	μ	ῳ	κ	ο	σ	μ
8. earth-D, gospel-N	γ	ῆ	α	ι	ε	ὐ	α	γ	γ	έ	λ	ι	ο	ν	γ	ῇ	π	ρ	ο	σ
9. child-D, day-N	τ	ε	κ	τ	τ	έ	κ	ν	ῳ	ο	υ	ἡ	μ	έ	ρ	α	μ	ε	ρ	α
10. law-N, soul-G	ψ	υ	χ	ῆ	ψ	υ	χ	ῆ	ς	ψ	υ	ν	ό	μ	ο	ς	ν	ό	μ	υ
11. day-D, word-A	λ	ο	γ	ο	ἡ	μ	έ	ρ	ᾳ	ο	ι	λ	ό	γ	ο	ν	μ	ε	ρ	ψ
12. law-A, temple-G	ι	ε	ρ	ο	ν	ό	μ	ο	ν	ο	μ	ἱ	ε	ρ	ο	ῦ	ρ	ω	ρ	σ
13. earth-D, life-N, work-N	π	ρ	ο	θ	γ	ῇ	ζ	ω	ή	α	ι	ἔ	ρ	γ	ο	ν	ε	ρ	ρ	γ
14. soul-N	α	ψ	ο	π	ψ	υ	χ	ῆ	ψ	υ	χ	ή	ν	β	ψ	υ	χ	ῆ	ς	π
15. God-A	λ	υ	π	ρ	θ	ε	ό	ς	β	θ	ε	ό	ν	ε	ο	χ	θ	ε	ο	ῦ
16. life-G	λ	ο	γ	ο	ψ	α	ζ	ω	ή	ν	ζ	ω	ῆ	ς	β	δ	ω	ι	κ	λ
17. deed-G	ε	ρ	γ	γ	ο	ἔ	ρ	γ	ῳ	ἔ	ρ	γ	ο	υ	ἔ	ρ	γ	ο	ν	ν
18. heart-N	κ	α	ρ	δ	ἱ	ᾳ	κ	κ	α	ρ	δ	ἱ	α	λ	α	μ	β	δ	α	α
19. face-D	π	ρ	ο	σ	σ	π	ρ	ο	σ	ώ	π	ῳ	π	ρ	ό	σ	ω	π	ο	ν
20. kingdom-A	β	α	β	α	σ	ι	λ	ε	ί	α	ν	β	α	σ	ι	λ	ε	ί	α	β

Lesson 4: Vocative Case

We've learned four cases so far: nominative, accusative, genitive and dative. Now it's time to learn the last case you need to know – the vocative case. The **vocative** is for **direct address**; it's used for any noun or pronoun in which someone (or something – like an animal or an object) is being directly spoken to. This lesson is just one page long, so you're going to love it!

Examples of the vocative in English

We've underlined some vocative nouns and pronouns in the English sentences below.

> **You,** there! Bring me my sword!
> Our **Father**, who art in heaven, hallowed be Thy name.
> **Friend**, lend me three loaves of bread.
> **Beloved**, let us cleanse ourselves from all defilement...
> Oh, my **soul**, why are you so downcast within me?
> **Lord**, did we not cast out demons in your name?

Examples of the vocative in Greek

Here are a few examples of the vocative case in Greek nouns you know.

...θεέ μου, ἵνα τί με ἐγκατέλιπες...	...my **God**, why have you forsaken me? *Mt. 27:46*
...Κύριε, οὐκ εἰμὶ ἱκανὸς...	...**Lord**, I am not worthy... *Mt. 8:8*
...Ἄνθρωπε, οὐκ οἶδα ὃ λέγεις....	...**man**, I don't know what you are saying. *Lk. 22:60*
... Ἀδελφέ, ἄφες ἐκβάλω τὸ κάρφος...	...**brother**, let me remove the speck... *Lk. 6:42*
...Θάρσει, τέκνον...	...take courage, **son**... *Mt. 9:2*
...Καὶ σύ, Βηθλέεμ γῆ Ἰούδα...	...and you, Bethlehem, **land** of Judah... *Mt. 2:6*
...καὶ ἐρῶ τῇ ψυχῇ μου Ψυχή,...	...and I will say to my soul, '**Soul,**... *Lk. 12:19*

In these examples, you can probably see *something* of a pattern emerging. If the stem ends in **omicron, the vocative case ending will often** (but not always) **be epsilon.** If the stem ends in **alpha** or **eta, there is no special case ending for the vocative**; the vocative case form is always identical to the nominative case form. In any situation, you can easily discern the vocative case by its context in the sentence. If a person or thing is being directly addressed, it is in the vocative case.

Since there are no hard and fast rules for vocative patterns in *every* situation, we're not adding the vocative case to our paradigm.

Exercise 4.1 – Review the Five Cases

In this all-English exercise, imagine that the following sentences were originally translated from Greek. **Write the case of each underlined word** using the abbreviations N-nominative, G-genitive, D-dative, A-accusative, V-vocative. The first one is done for you as an example.

1 The **kingdom**   N   of **heaven**   G   belongs to You, O **Lord**   V   .

2 The **voice**_____ of the **prophet**_____ gives a **word**_____ to the **people**_____ .

3 **Heaven**_____ and **earth**_____ give **glory**_____ to **God**_____ .

4 The **Word**_____ is **truth**_____ .

5 **Christ**_____ in **heaven**_____ is the hope of the **resurrection**_____ .

6 The **child**_____ of **God**_____ loves the **brothers**_____ .

7 The **Spirit**_____ of **God**_____ lives in the **heart**_____ of the **believer**_____ .

8 **God**_____ is in the **temple**_____ .

9 How long, **son**_____, will you resist confessing **sin**_____?

10 The **law**_____ of **God**_____ is holy.

─────────────── A N S W E R   K E Y ───────────────

1. N, G, V   6. N, G, A
2. N, G, A, D   7. N, G, D, G
3. N, N, A, D   8. N, D
4. N, N   9. V, A
5. N, D, G   10. N, G

Lesson 5: Plural Forms

You've learned the endings for the five cases of the majority of **singular** nouns whose stems end in omicron, alpha and eta. But, what about their **plural** forms? It's time to learn them now.

We're going to do something a little unusual for our style of teaching. We're going to "throw you in over your head" by showing you the complete paradigm with all the case endings, both singular and plural. The reason we can do this is because – believe it or not – you are ready to swim.

We've revised the paradigm to accommodate plural forms. The top half is for the singular forms. The bottom half is for the plural forms. Take a look!

The paradigm for singular and plural nouns whose stems end in omicron, alpha or eta

Important: Letter shaded in gray means that the final stem vowel *changes* to that vowel.

	masculine nouns *whose stems end in omicron (o)*	feminine nouns *whose stems end in alpha or eta (α , η)*	neuter nouns *whose stems end in omicron (o)*
nominative singular	ς	–	ν
genitive singular	υ	ς	υ
dative singular	ι*	ι*	ι*
accusative singular	ν	ν	ν

nominative plural	ι	ι	α
genitive plural	ων	ων	ων
dative plural	ις	ις	ις
accusative plural	υς	ς	α

* In the dative *singular*, the final stem vowel *lengthens* and the iota *subscripts*. We've indicated this situation with an asterisk. However, in the dative *plural*, the final stem vowel does *not* lengthen and the iota does *not* subscript. It's just a regular iota.

Now, we're going to show you actual words in the paradigm, so you can see the case ending patterns a little better.

Paradigm of noun case form examples

	masculine nouns *whose stems end in omicron (o)*	feminine nouns *whose stems end in alpha or eta*		neuter nouns *whose stems end in omicron (o)*
		(α)	*(η)*	
nom sg	λόγος	καρδία	φωνή	ἔργον
gen sg	λόγου	καρδίας¹	φωνῆς	ἔργου
dat sg	λόγῳ	καρδίᾳ	φωνῇ	ἔργῳ
acc sg	λόγον	καρδίαν	φωνήν	ἔργον
nom pl	λόγοι	καρδίαι	φωναί	ἔργα³
gen pl	λόγων³	καρδιῶν³	φωνῶν³	ἔργων³
dat pl	λόγοις	καρδίαις	φωναῖς²	ἔργοις
acc pl	λόγους	καρδίας¹	φωνάς²	ἔργα³

¹ Note that, for feminine nouns whose stems end in alpha, the genitive singular and accusative plural forms are identical. This is an example of an "unhelpful" ending. However, we will teach you the definite article soon, and that will often clear up any ambiguity between these two cases. Take a look at the neuter nouns, while you're at it. See how the nominative plural and accusative plural forms look identical? Another pair with an unhelpful ending. (Actually, there are *three* pairs of unhelpful endings in this chart. The third pair is the one you already learned about in past lessons – the neuter nominative singular and accusative singular forms.)

² Note the stem vowel change from eta to alpha in the dative plural and accusative plural forms. This does happen; don't be alarmed about it. It's actually a nice feature in stems ending with eta, because it prevents that "unhelpful ending" situation from occurring.

³ The final stem vowel actually changes to an entirely different vowel for these cases.

The vocative plural is identical to the nominative plural

The vocative case is not included in our paradigm above. Just so you know, **the vocative plural form is identical to the nominative plural form.** So, if a scripture has, "Brothers, listen to me," the word *brothers* is in the vocative case and is spelled exactly like the nominative plural form: ἄνθρωποι.

Big-time terminology

Now that you've witnessed your first paradigm of both singular and plural forms, we hope you are not too dismayed. It looks like a lot, and it *is* a lot, but you don't have to memorize it all right now. You can refer to the chart as often as you like for all the exercises in this book. You'll be grateful for the next lesson, when we can finally show you the definite article. The definite article, together with the paradigm on the previous page, will *really* help you identify noun cases in a verse of scripture.

Now... We would not be doing a good job if we didn't teach you some official, big-time terminology at this point in your studies. If you use any other Greek textbooks or reference tools, you are going to run into these terms, so you'll need to know what they mean. Caution: If you go around saying these terms out loud in the presence of normal people, you'll really sound like a "Greek geek." You might want to keep these under your hat.

Declining, Declension and Inflection

Let's start with the term *decline*. Believe it or not, you've been learning to *decline* nouns ever since you started using this workbook! To **decline** a noun simply means "to list the various forms of a noun." Example sentences using this verb:

> Dang! My Greek teacher is making us **decline** forty nouns for homework tonight!
> Most Greek nouns **decline** into at least eight distinct forms.

This leads us to a related term, *declension*. The term *declension* is just the noun form of the verb *to decline*. A **declension** is "a spelling pattern for the different forms of a noun." In English, toddlers who want to form plurals must learn at least two different declensions:

> Declension 1: Add an "s" to the end of nouns that are amenable to receiving a simple "s" ending – such as words that don't *already* end in an "s" sound.

> Declension 2: Add an "es" to the end of nouns that *aren't* amenable to receiving a simple "s" – such as words already ending in "s," or words ending in "x" or "ch."

You've already learned two different declensions in Greek nouns, although up until now, we haven't *called* them declensions. Not surprisingly, the first two declensions (which you have already learned) are called First Declension and Second Declension. There's even a Third Declension (which we haven't taught you yet). **Here are Greek's three declensions:**

> **First Declension**: A spelling pattern for nouns whose stems end in **alpha** or **eta**.

> **Second Declension**: A spelling pattern for nouns whose stems end in **omicron**.

> **Third Declension**: A spelling pattern for nouns whose stems end in a **consonant**.

All right. The last term you need to know is the term **inflection**. In grammar, **inflection** is **a change in the form of a word** (typically the ending) **which is made in order to express a particular grammatical attribute**. Inflection can express all sorts of attributes, such as *tense, case, voice, person, aspect, number, gender* and *mood*. You've been observing inflections of *case, number* and *gender* throughout this book. Every time a noun changes spelling because of a grammatical attribute, that's called an "inflection."

Some languages are "highly inflected." "Highly inflected" means that nearly all their words will change spellings, depending on the grammatical attributes listed above. Such languages include Greek, Latin, Romance languages (Spanish, Italian, French, Portuguese, Romanian), German and Biblical Hebrew.

Some languages are "weakly inflected," like English. This means that certain changes in spelling *can* occur, but not always. English verbs will change forms for certain attributes (like *tense* and *number*) but not for other attributes (like *gender*). English nouns will change forms for an attribute like *number*, but not for attributes like *case* or *gender*.

Some languages never use inflections at all. One example is Mandarin Chinese. This is why some native Mandarin speakers struggle with things like verb tenses when they first try to learn English. They don't even *have* different forms for their verbs. Each Mandarin Chinese verb just has *one* form for every tense – whether past, present or future. And their nouns don't decline, either. In Mandarin, you just use the same word to say either "dog" or "dogs."

Why Greek nouns hate going to the doctor

Alternate declension patterns

Certain Greek nouns whose stems end in alpha will experience a change in stem vowel to eta in the genitive singular and dative singular case. It looks a little strange; we didn't want you to be startled by it. There is actually a rule about when this shift can occur. It only happens when the letter before the stem vowel is *not* epsilon, iota or rho. Only a few such words occur with enough frequency in the New Testament that you need to be concerned about them. One example you'll certainly encounter is δόξα (glory, majesty, fame). We highlighted its alpha-to-eta shift.

δόξα	*nominative/vocative singular*	δόξαι	*nominative/vocative plural*
δόξης	*genitive singular*	δοξῶν	*genitive plural*
δόξῃ	*dative singular*	δόξαις	*dative plural*
δόξαν	*accusative singular*	δόξας	*accusative plural*

Do *all* nouns decline? What about proper nouns?

Some Greek nouns don't decline fully. This means these nouns might have four or less forms rather than eight or more. Partial declension happens frequently with proper nouns.

The declension of the name "Jesus"

The name Jesus (or Joshua) is partially declined, because, as you'd expect, there are no plural forms. Here's the declension:

Ἰησοῦς	*nominative singular*
Ἰησοῦ	*genitive singular*
Ἰησοῦ	*dative singular*
Ἰησοῦν	*accusative singular*

Notice that the genitive and dative forms are identical. The easiest way to discern between those two cases in a verse of scripture is to pay attention to the definite article (which we'll be teaching you in the next lesson). Definite articles usually precede proper names in Greek.

A Mandarin noun party?
Gee, thanks for inviting me, but...
I'm Greek. I have to decline.

Μάρκος

劉

Examples of plural nouns in scripture

Now that we've gotten that terminology out of the way, how about we look at some real examples of plural nouns from scripture? We've highlighted them in gray. We've also included the bottom half of the paradigm showing just the **plural** case endings, for your convenience. Take a moment now to locate where each gray-highlighted word should fit in the paradigm chart. Think about each word's grammatical function in the sentence and see how its case ending is appropriate.

	masculine nouns *whose stems end in omicron (o)*	feminine nouns *whose stems end in alpha or eta (α , η)*	neuter nouns *whose stems end in omicron (o)*
nominative plural	ι	ι	α
genitive plural	ων	ων	ων
dative plural	ις	ις	ις
accusative plural	υς	ς	α

... εἰσὶν θεοὶ πολλοὶ καὶ κύριοι πολλοί...   ...there are many **gods** and many **lords**... *1 Cor. 8:5*

...διδοὺς νόμους μου εἰς τὴν διάνοιαν αὐτῶν...   ...putting My **laws** in their mind... *Heb. 8:10*

...καὶ διαλογιζόμενοι ἐν ταῖς καρδίαις αὐτῶν...   ...and reasoning in their **hearts**... *Mk. 2:6*

...τοσαῦτα εἰ τύχοι γένη φωνῶν εἰσιν...   ...There are...many kinds of **voices**... *1 Cor. 14:10*

...ἐπιστηρίζοντες τὰς ψυχὰς...   ...strengthening the **souls**... *Acts 14:22*

...δόματα ἀγαθὰ διδόναι τοῖς τέκνοις...   ...to give good gifts to the **children**... *Mt. 7:11*

...ἦν γὰρ αὐτῶν πονηρὰ τὰ ἔργα....   ...indeed their **deeds** were evil... *Jn. 3:19*

...ὑμεῖς ποιεῖτε τὰ ἔργα τοῦ πατρὸς ὑμῶν...   ...you are doing the **deeds** of your father... *Jn. 8:41*

Exercise 5.1 – Scripture Match Up

Fill in the blanks of actual scripture using the correct form of each noun. The Word Banks contain your possible choices. Be sure to read the entire verse to discern the noun's function in the sentence so that you'll know which case form to choose. Refer to your paradigms as often as you need to. Answers are at the bottom of each page. In the answer keys, we also provide explanatory abbreviations such as AMP (accusative masculine plural), GNP (genitive neuter plural), etc.

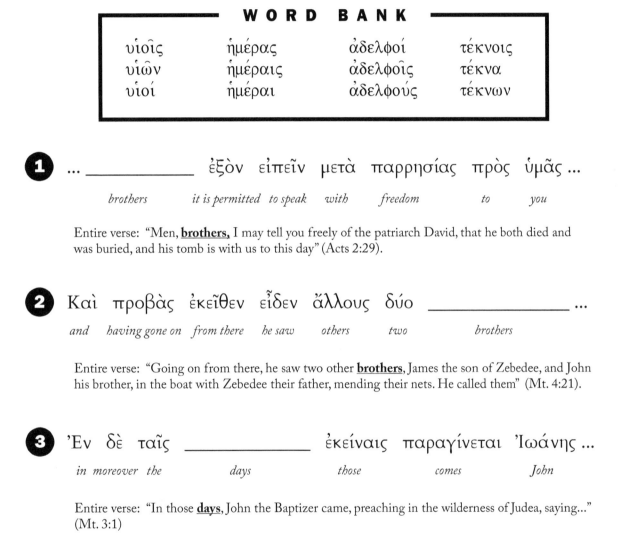

```
┌──────────────── W O R D   B A N K ────────────────┐
│                                                    │
│   υἱοῖς        ἡμέρας       ἀδελφοί      τέκνοις    │
│   υἱῶν         ἡμέραις      ἀδελφοῖς     τέκνα      │
│   υἱοί         ἡμέραι       ἀδελφούς     τέκνων     │
│                                                    │
└────────────────────────────────────────────────────┘
```

1 ... _____ ἐξὸν εἰπεῖν μετὰ παρρησίας πρὸς ὑμᾶς ...

    brothers   it is permitted to speak with   freedom   to   you

Entire verse: "Men, **brothers,** I may tell you freely of the patriarch David, that he both died and was buried, and his tomb is with us to this day" (Acts 2:29).

2 Καὶ προβὰς ἐκεῖθεν εἶδεν ἄλλους δύο _____ ...

    and   having gone on from there he saw others   two   brothers

Entire verse: "Going on from there, he saw two other **brothers,** James the son of Zebedee, and John his brother, in the boat with Zebedee their father, mending their nets. He called them" (Mt. 4:21).

3 Ἐν δὲ ταῖς _____ ἐκείναις παραγίνεται Ἰωάνης ...

    in moreover the   days   those   comes   John

Entire verse: "In those **days,** John the Baptizer came, preaching in the wilderness of Judea, saying..." (Mt. 3:1)

4 ἐλεύσονται δὲ _____ ὅταν ἀπαρθῇ ἀπ' αὐτῶν ὁ νυμφίος...

    will come moreover days   when will have been from   them   the bridegroom
                                 taken away

Entire verse: "But the **days** will come when the bridegroom will be taken away from them, and then will they fast in that day" (Mk. 2:20).

Exercise 5.1 – Scripture Match Up, *continued*

```
┌─────────── W O R D   B A N K ───────────┐
│   υἱοῖς       καρδίας       ψυχαῖς      τέκνοις   │
│   υἱῶν        καρδίαις      ψυχάς       τέκνα     │
│   υἱοί        καρδιῶν       ψυχαί       τέκνων    │
└─────────────────────────────────────────┘
```

5 ...Ὅτι δέ ἐστε _____, ἐξαπέστειλεν ὁ Θεὸς...

because moreover you are   sons,   sent forth   -   God

Entire verse: "And because you are **sons**, God sent out the Spirit of his Son into your hearts, crying, 'Abba, Father!'" (Gal. 4:6)

6 ...καὶ πᾶσαν τὴν γερουσίαν τῶν _____ Ἰσραήλ...

and   all   the   senate   of the   sons   of Israel

Entire verse: "When they heard this, they entered into the temple about daybreak, and taught. But the high priest came, and those who were with him, and called the council together, and all the senate of the **sons** of Israel, and sent to the prison to have them brought" (Acts 5:21).

7 ...καὶ εὑρήσετε ἀνάπαυσιν ταῖς _____ ὑμῶν.

and   you will find   rest   [for] the   souls   of you

Entire verse: "Take my yoke upon you, and learn from me, for I am gentle and lowly in heart; and you will find rest for your **souls**" (Mt. 11:29). *Important hint: In Greek, the literal wording is "rest for the souls of you," in which "souls" is acting purely as an indirect object (no concept of possession), while the "of you" is a distinct part of the phrase, in the genitive case, which carries the concept of the possessive "your."*

8 ...εἶδον ὑποκάτω τοῦ θυσιαστηρίου τὰς _____...

I saw   under   the   altar   the   souls

Entire verse: "When he opened the fifth seal, I saw underneath the altar the **souls** of those who had been killed for the Word of God, and for the testimony of the Lamb which they had" (Rev. 6:9).

Answers: 5. υἱοί (NMP) **6.** υἱῶν (GMP) **7.** ψυχαῖς (DFP) **8.** ψυχάς (AFP). Don't be concerned about the accent mark changing from acute to grave on some of these spellings; such changes are governed by the spellings of the words which follow them in the verse.

Exercise 5.1 – Scripture Match Up, *continued*

```
┌─────────────── W O R D   B A N K ───────────────┐
│                                                 │
│   υἱοῖς       καρδίας      ψυχαῖς      τέκνοις   │
│   υἱῶν        καρδίαις     ψυχάς       τέκνα     │
│   υἱοί        καρδιῶν      ψυχαί       τέκνων    │
│                                                 │
└─────────────────────────────────────────────────┘
```

9 ... ἄνθρωπος   εἶχεν   _____   δύο....

    a man   *had*   *children*   *two*

Entire verse: "But what do you think? A man had two **children**, and he came to the first, and said, 'Child, go work today in my vineyard'" (Mt. 21:28). *Note: The literal word in Greek is "children," but in this parable's context it is usually translated into English Bibles as "sons."*

10 ...Οὐκ   ἔστιν   καλὸν   λαβεῖν   τὸν   ἄρτον   τῶν   _____...

    not   *it is*   *right*   *to take*   *the*   *bread*   *of the*   *children*

Entire verse: "But he answered, 'It is not appropriate to take the **children's** bread and throw it to the dogs'" (Mt. 15:26).

11 ...Σκληροτράχηλοι   καὶ   ἀπερίτμητοι   _____   καὶ   τοῖς   ὠσίν...

    you stiff-necked   *and*   *uncircumcised*   *in hearts*   *and*   *ears*

Entire verse: "You stiff-necked and uncircumcised in **heart** and ears, you always resist the Holy Spirit! As your fathers did, so you do" (Acts 7:51). *Note: In the original Greek, the word translated here "heart" is actually plural, "hearts"; literally it reads, "uncircumcised in hearts and ears." It is never considered correct English to say "in hearts," so the translators were required to modify the word in the English. This kind of compromise happens frequently when translating between any two languages.*

12 ...ἐγώ   εἰμι   ὁ   ἐραυνῶν   νεφροὺς   καὶ   _____...

    I   *am*   *the*   *searching*   *affections*   *and*   *hearts*

Entire verse: "I will kill her children with Death, and all the assemblies will know that I am he who searches the minds and **hearts**. I will give to each one of you according to your deeds" (Rev. 2:23).

Answers: 9. τέκνα (ANP)   10. τέκνων (GNP)   11. καρδίαις (DFP)   12. καρδίας (AFP).

Would you like a chart showing the four case forms for all the nouns you've been studying in both **singular** and **plural** forms? This chart spans two pages.

	nom. sg.	gen. sg.	dat. sg.	acc. sg.	meaning
masculine nouns stems ending in omicron	θεός	θεοῦ	θεῷ	θεόν	*God, god*
	κύριος	κυρίου	κυρίῳ	κύριον	*Lord, lord, master*
	ἄνθρωπος	ἀνθρώπου	ἀνθρώπῳ	ἄνθρωπον	*man, humankind*
	Χριστός	Χριστοῦ	Χριστῷ	Χριστόν	*Christ, anointed one*
	υἱός	υἱοῦ	υἱῷ	υἱόν	*son, descendant*
	ἀδελφός	ἀδελφοῦ	ἀδελφῷ	ἀδελφόν	*brother*
	λόγος	λόγου	λόγῳ	λόγον	*word, statement*
	οὐρανός	οὐρανοῦ	οὐρανῷ	οὐρανόν	*heaven, sky*
	νόμος	νόμου	νόμῳ	νόμον	*law, principle*
	κόσμος	κόσμου	κόσμῳ	κόσμον	*world, universe*
feminine nouns stems ending in alpha	ἡμέρα	ἡμέρας	ἡμέρᾳ	ἡμέραν	*day*
	καρδία	καρδίας	καρδίᾳ	καρδίαν	*heart, inner self*
	βασιλεία	βασιλείας	βασιλείᾳ	βασιλείαν	*kingdom, sovereignty*
	ἁμαρτία	ἁμαρτίας	ἁμαρτίᾳ	ἁμαρτίαν	*sin, moral failure*
feminine nouns stems ending in eta	γῆ	γῆς	γῇ	γῆν	*earth, land*
	φωνή	φωνῆς	φωνῇ	φωνήν	*sound, voice, noise*
	ζωή	ζωῆς	ζωῇ	ζωήν	*life*
	ψυχή	ψυχῆς	ψυχῇ	ψυχήν	*soul, breath, life*
neuter nouns stems ending in omicron	ἔργον	ἔργου	ἔργῳ	ἔργον	*work, deed, act*
	τέκνον	τέκνου	τέκνῳ	τέκνον	*child, descendant*
	σημεῖον	σημείου	σημείῳ	σημεῖον	*sign, miracle*
	εὐαγγέλιον	εὐαγγελίου	εὐαγγελίῳ	εὐαγγέλιον	*good news, gospel*
	πρόσωπον	προσώπου	προσώπῳ	πρόσωπον	*face, appearance*
	ἱερόν	ἱεροῦ	ἱερῷ	ἱερόν	*temple*

	nom. pl.	gen. pl.	dat. pl.	acc. pl.	meaning
masculine nouns stems ending in omicron	θεοί	θεῶν	θεοῖς	θεούς	*gods*
	κύριοι	κυρίων	κυρίοις	κυρίους	*lords, masters*
	ἄνθρωποι	ἀνθρώπων	ἀνθρώποις	ἀνθρώπους	*men, humankind*
	unused*	unused	unused	unused	*anointed ones*
	υἱοί	υἱῶν	υἱοῖς	υἱούς	*sons, descendants*
	ἀδελφοί	ἀδελφῶν	ἀδελφοῖς	ἀδελφούς	*brothers*
	λόγοι	λόγων	λόγοις	λόγους	*words, statements*
	οὐρανοί	οὐρανῶν	οὐρανοῖς	οὐρανούς	*heavens, skies*
	unused	unused	unused	νόμους	*laws, principles*
	unused	unused	unused	unused	*worlds*
feminine nouns stems ending in alpha	ἡμέραι	ἡμερῶν	ἡμέραις	ἡμέρας	*days*
	καρδίαι	καρδιῶν	καρδίαις	καρδίας	*hearts, inner selves*
	unused	unused	unused	βασιλείας	*kingdoms, sovereignties*
	ἁμαρτίαι	ἁμαρτιῶν	ἁμαρτίαις	ἁμαρτίας	*sins, moral failures*
feminine nouns stems ending in eta	unused	unused	unused	unused	*earths, lands*
	φωναί	φωνῶν	φωναῖς	φωνάς	*sounds, voices, noises*
	unused	unused	unused	unused	*lives*
	ψυχαί	ψυχῶν	ψυχαῖς	ψυχάς	*souls, breaths, lives*
neuter nouns stems ending in omicron	ἔργα	ἔργων	ἔργοις	ἔργα	*works, deeds, acts*
	τέκνα	τέκνων	τέκνοις	τέκνα	*children, descendants*
	σημεῖα	σημείων	σημείοις	σημεῖα	*signs, miracles*
	unused	unused	unused	unused	*gospels*
	πρόσωπα	προσώπων	unused	πρόσωπα	*faces, appearances*
	unused	unused	unused	unused	*temples*

* "Unused" means this form is not used (or is very rarely used) in the Greek of the New Testament.

Jim and Lisa Cummins are probably more relieved to be done with Lesson 5 than the students are.

Lesson 6: The Article

In English, we have parts of speech called "articles" which are placed before nouns. English has two types of articles: **indefinite** ("a" or "an") and **definite** ("the"). The indefinite articles "a" or "an" imply the speaker **does not know, or is not attempting to indicate,** the exact identity to which the noun refers. The definite article "the" implies the speaker or writer **"definitely" knows, or "definitely" is attempting to indicate,** the exact identity to which the noun refers. Here are some English examples of the indefinite and definite article:

1. Police say the man may be hiding in **a** house on the south side of the city. *(indefinite)*
2. This is **the** house my father built with his own hands. *(definite)*

In the first sentence, the speaker wasn't "definite" about which house the man was hiding in, so he used the indefinite article "a". In the second sentence, the speaker was "definite" about which house he was referring to, so he used the definite article "the."

Greek has no indefinite article

In Greek, there is no indefinite article. If you come across examples such as the following, you are expected to insert the words "a" or "an" as necessary when you translate it into English. Notice how each phrase below begins with one of your vocabulary words, but lacks any sort of article representing "a" or "an." (You should focus only on the underlined words in these phrases, because we haven't taught you any of the other words yet.)

<u>πνεῦμα</u> λαμβάνει αὐτόν   "**<u>a spirit</u>** seizes him" (Lk 9:39)

<u>ἀνὴρ</u> ἔστη ἐνώπιόν μου   "**<u>a man</u>** stood before me" (Acts 10:30)

<u>γυνὴ</u> οὖσα ἐν ῥύσει αἵματος   "**<u>a woman</u>** having a hemorrhage (Lk 8:43)

It will be your responsibility as a translator to add the words "a" or "an" into your English phrases when needed. Sometimes you'll think it best to omit the "a" or "an" entirely. For example, while it may be technically accurate to translate a phrase as "they ate a supper," it feels more natural in English (and is just as accurate) to say "they ate supper" (without any article).

Greek has a definite article

What about when the item being discussed is *definite*? Thankfully, **Greek *does* have a definite article**, and, since it is the *only* kind of article in Greek, it is often simply called "the article." (It's not *wrong* to call it "the definite article," though.) The Greek article takes many different forms (spellings), depending on the **gender, number** and **case** of whatever noun it precedes. This requirement to match the form of the article with the form of the noun paired with it is called **agreement**. In other words, the article must **agree** with the noun with which it is paired.

Agreement in English

To better illustrate what we mean by "agreement," let's look at a few examples in the English language. Notice how certain of our words change form (spelling) in order to "agree" with the nouns they modify.

this woman	"this" (singular form) agrees with "woman" (singular form)
these women	"these" (plural form) agrees with "women" (plural form)
he **says**	"says" (singular form) agrees with "he" (singular form)
they **say**	"say" (plural form) agrees with "they" (plural form)

Now, you'll notice that our articles *a, an* and *the* never change form at all. No matter what kind of noun they are paired with – plural or singular, masculine or feminine – they are always spelled the same way. Not so in Greek.

Agreement with the Greek definite article

Greek is a bit more complex than English, because Greek nouns have more than just **number** to worry about (singular vs. plural). They also need to agree in **gender** and **case**. This means there are many different forms of the Greek article.

Guess what? We have another paradigm to help you. This time, it's a handy paradigm of all the forms of the Greek article. This chart will make it easy for you to use the correct form to agree with each noun in your exercises. You'll also find this paradigm extremely useful for discerning which case a noun is in, especially when you're dealing with those pesky, "unhelpful" case endings.

Take a moment now to look carefully over the paradigm on the following page. **If you are able to memorize things, we urge you to memorize the paradigm on the following page**. If memorization is very difficult or impossible for you, then make a copy of the page and use it as a bookmark for all your Greek studies, like a cheat sheet.

We promise that these facts about the definite article will come into play in *every* passage of Greek scripture you ever try to interpret, so the return on your time investment to learn the paradigm will be huge! The Greek article appears more than 20,000 times in the New Testament. So, just by learning the 24 forms on the next page, you'll be able to instantly recognize 14.5% of all the words in the Greek scriptures. The grammatical information revealed by these forms is going to be even more of a bonus for your scriptural studies. Go for it!

The paradigm for the forms of the article

	masculine	feminine	neuter
nominative singular	ὁ *hah*	ἡ *hay*	τό *tah*
genitive singular	τοῦ *too*	τῆς *tayss*	τοῦ *too*
dative singular	τῷ *tōh[1]*	τῇ *tay*	τῷ *tōh*
accusative singular	τόν *tahn[2]*	τήν *tayn*	τό *tah*

	masculine	feminine	neuter
nominative plural	οἱ *hoy*	αἱ *hai[3]*	τά *tah*
genitive plural	τῶν *tōhn[4]*	τῶν *tōhn*	τῶν *tōhn*
dative plural	τοῖς *toyss*	ταῖς *taiss[5]*	τοῖς *toyss*
accusative plural	τούς *tooss*	τάς *tahss*	τά *tah*

[1] τῷ *tōh* rhymes with *go*. It must be pronounced with that long ō sound. Now, you should be aware that many people *also* pronounce the neuter nominative singular form, τό, so it rhymes with "go," but they "clip" their voice, spending less time saying the syllable. That's how they differentiate the "short" omicron from the "long" omega. Omicron is pronounced in slightly different ways by different people, depending on where they studied Greek. Remember that our workbook series represents just *one* of the acceptable "seminary pronunciation" systems.

[2] τόν *tahn* is acceptable, but, again, some people lean toward a long ō sound, making it sound more like *tone*.

[3] αἱ *hai* rhymes with *goodbye*. It is pronounced just like the "Hi!" we use in greeting.

[4] τῶν *tōhn* sounds <u>exactly</u> like *tone*. (This one <u>definitely</u> has the long ō sound, because of the omega.)

[5] ταῖς *taiss* rhymes with *mice* or *dice*.

All the above forms are translated "<u>the</u>." At least, they *usually* are. Sometimes the article is translated with an additional preposition such as <u>in the</u>, <u>of the</u> or <u>to the</u>. The article actually gets a wide variety of translations. For now, you can think of the article as simply meaning "<u>the</u>."

Now... a couple noteworthy items:

First – and most awesome – the forms of the article in this paradigm represent *all* the possible spellings of the Greek word "<u>the</u>." **There aren't any other spellings to learn. This is it.** That's because these forms ignore declensions. The Greek article only cares about *three* things when it wants to agree with a noun: the noun's *gender*, *number* and *case*. The article doesn't seem to care that stems even *exist*, never mind what vowels the stems end in. (That's why this paradigm doesn't list the usual restrictions about "stems ending in omicron," "stems ending in alpha," etc.)

Second, **notice the rough breathing marks in four of the forms.** They're easy to miss. That's why we included transliterations in this particular paradigm – to help you notice the "h" sounds.

Let's see some of these article forms in action, why don't we? The paradigm below will make it abundantly clear how the article *agrees* with the noun following it.

Paradigm of noun case form examples with the article

	masculine nouns	feminine nouns		neuter nouns
nom sg	ὁ λόγος *the word*	ἡ καρδία *the heart*	ἡ φωνή *the voice*	τὸ ἔργον *the work*
gen sg	τοῦ λόγου *the word*	τῆς καρδίας *the heart*	τῆς φωνῆς *the voice*	τοῦ ἔργου *the work*
dat sg	τῷ λόγῳ *the word*	τῇ καρδίᾳ *the heart*	τῇ φωνῇ *the voice*	τῷ ἔργῳ *the work*
acc sg	τὸν λόγον *the word*	τὴν καρδίαν *the heart*	τὴν φωνήν *the voice*	τὸ ἔργον *the work*

	masculine nouns	feminine nouns		neuter nouns
nom pl	οἱ λόγοι *the words*	αἱ καρδίαι *the hearts*	αἱ φωναί *the voices*	τὰ ἔργα *the works*
gen pl	τῶν λόγων *the words*	τῶν καρδιῶν *the hearts*	τῶν φωνῶν *the voices*	τῶν ἔργων *the works*
dat pl	τοῖς λόγοις *the words*	ταῖς καρδίαις *the hearts*	ταῖς φωναῖς *the voices*	τοῖς ἔργοις *the works*
acc pl	τοὺς λόγους *the words*	τὰς καρδίας *the hearts*	τὰς φωνάς *the voices*	τὰ ἔργα *the works*

Times when you don't translate the definite article

There are times when Greek will use the definite article in front of a word, yet it would be unnecessary, wrong, or awkward to include it in English. One example is Greek's insistent use of definite articles in front of proper names, like the name "Jesus." For example, Matthew 3:13 has:

Τότε παραγίνεται ὁ Ἰησοῦς ἀπὸ τῆς Γαλιλαίας ἐπὶ τὸν Ἰορδάνην...

Literally, this says, "Then comes **the** Jesus from **the** Galilee to **the** Jordan." Most English Bible translations have something like: "Then Jesus came from Galilee to the Jordan." Translators must make any changes appropriate to the standards of the English language.

Why the definite article is so helpful

We've been promising you all along that the Greek article could really help you out of a jam. On the paradigm on the preceding page, there are a few examples of unhelpful case endings on some of the nouns. Here's an example.

heart, genitive singular	καρδίας
hearts, accusative plural	καρδίας

Very unhelpful. The forms are identical. If you ran across these in scripture, how would you know which case was intended? You'd have to use the context to the best of your ability. Now, take a look at some actual examples of these two forms from scripture.

τῇ πωρώσει τῆς καρδίας	the hardness of the **heart**... (Mk. 3:5)
Θεὸς γινώσκει τὰς καρδίας	God knows the **hearts**... (Lk. 16:15)

The top scripture shows the noun "heart" in the *genitive singular* case. The bottom scripture shows it in *accusative plural*. Of course, the *cases* may be evident from the context, and the *numbers* are certainly evident from the English translations. But, what if you had no translations to help you? Take a good look at the *articles*. This time, they are also highlighted in gray.

τῇ πωρώσει τῆς καρδίας	the hardness of **the heart**... (Mk. 3:5)
Θεὸς γινώσκει τὰς καρδίας	God knows **the hearts**... (Lk. 16:15)

See how the article always agrees with and exposes the noun's true case? Not only that, but it also reveals the noun's *number*. Why is this useful? Here's an example. In English, the word "heart" is often translated in singular form even though the Greek has it in plural form. If a Greek scripture literally has, "Blessed are *you* (plural), pure in the *hearts* (plural)," it is translated, "Blessed are you, pure in heart." In English, the word "heart" gets changed into *singular* form in the phrase "pure in heart" – which could just as easily mean "one person's heart" as "many people's hearts." Similarly, the English word "you" is ambiguous as to whether it is singular or plural, since English uses just one form, "you," for both situations. The process of translating to English inadvertently results in "losing" or "hiding" some of the important grammar data of the original Greek.

You have all the tools to be a good detective

You now have access to the grammar data of the Greek article and many nouns. Just use *all* the tools in your toolbox. First, get a feel for the **whole context** of the chapter (read it in an English translation). Then, looking at the Greek verse, think about the **noun's grammatical function**. Look at the **noun's case ending**, and refer to a paradigm to verify the case. If there's an **article** before the noun, study its **form**. All these clues together will give you a clear understanding.

Exercise 6.1 – Choose the Article

Fill in the blanks of actual scripture below using the correct form of the article. Hint: look at the case ending of the noun following the article, determine its case, gender and number, and then choose the article form which agrees. If the ending is unhelpful, then think about the noun's function in the sentence. Refer to your paradigms as often as you need to. Answers are at the bottom of the page. In the answers, we provide explanatory case-gender-number abbreviations, too.

1 ...διήρχετο   δὲ   μᾶλλον _____ λόγος περὶ αὐτοῦ...

was spread abroad moreover still more   the   word   about   him

Entire verse: "But **the** report concerning him spread much more, and great multitudes came together to hear, and to be healed by him of their infirmities" (Lk. 5:15).

2 ...καὶ   ὑπηρέται   γενόμενοι _____ λόγου...

and   servants   having been   (of) the   word

Entire verse: "...even as those who from the beginning were eyewitnesses and servants of **the** word delivered them to us..." (Lk. 1:2)

3 ... τὰ παθήματα ____ ἁμαρτιῶν τὰ διὰ ____ νόμου ἐνηργεῖτο...

the   passions   (of) the   sins   that through the   law   were at work

Entire verse: "For when we were in the flesh, **the** sinful passions which were through **the** law, worked in our members to bring forth fruit to death" (Rom. 7:5). *Hint: Literally, "the passions of the sins..."*

4 ... διεπρίοντο _____ καρδίαις αὐτῶν...

they were cut   (in) the   hearts   of them

Entire verse: "Now when they heard these things, they were cut to **the** heart, and they gnashed at him with their teeth" (Acts 7:54). *Hint: The literal translation is "they were cut in the hearts" (plural).*

Answers: 1. ὁ (NMS) 2. τοῦ (GMS) 3. τῶν (GFP), τοῦ (GMS) 4. ταῖς (DFP).

Exercise 6.1 – Choose the Article, *continued*

5 ...οὐχὶ _____ ψυχὴ πλεῖόν ἐστιν τῆς τροφῆς...

    not   *the*   *life*   *more*   *is*   *than the*   *food*

Entire verse: "Therefore, I tell you, don't be anxious for your life: what you will eat, or what you will drink; nor yet for your body, what you will wear. Isn't [**the***] life more than food, and the body more than clothing?" (Mt. 6:25)   *Note: the article is not translated into English in this particular case.*

6 ...ἐπιστηρίζοντες _____ ψυχὰς τῶν μαθητῶν...

    strengthening   *the*   *souls*   *of the*   *disciples*

Entire verse: "strengthening **the** souls of the disciples, exhorting them to continue in the faith, and that through many afflictions we must enter into the Kingdom of God" (Acts 14:22).

7 Καὶ προσῆλθον αὐτῷ τυφλοὶ καὶ χωλοὶ ἐν _____ ἱερῷ...

    and   *came*   *to him*   *blind*   *and*   *lame*   *in*   *the*   *temple*

Entire verse: "The blind and the lame came to him in **the** temple, and he healed them" (Mt. 21:14).

8 ὃς καὶ _____ ἱερὸν ἐπείρασεν βεβηλῶσαι...

    who   *even*   *the*   *temple*   *attempted*   *to profane*

Entire verse: "He even tried to profane **the** temple, and we arrested him" (Acts 24:6).

9 καὶ εἶπεν Ἰδοὺ θεωρῶ _____ οὐρανοὺς...

    and   *he said,*   *Behold*   *I see*   *the*   *heavens*

Entire verse: "and said, 'Behold, I see **the** heavens opened, and the Son of Man standing at the right hand of God!'" (Acts 7:56)

Answers: 5. ἡ (NFS) 6. τὰς (AFP) 7. τῷ (DNS) 8. τὸ (ANS) 9. τοὺς (AMP)

Exercise 6.1 – Choose the Article, *continued*

10 ...καὶ αἱ δυνάμεις αἱ ἐν _____ οὐρανοῖς σαλευθήσονται.

and   the   powers   that   in   the   heavens   will be shaken

Entire verse: "the stars will be falling from the sky, and the powers that are in **the** heavens will be shaken" (Mk. 13:25).

11 ...ὅτι κλείετε _____ βασιλείαν _____ οὐρανῶν...

for   you shut up   the   kingdom   (of) the   heavens

Entire verse: "Woe to you, scribes and Pharisees, hypocrites! For you shut up **the** kingdom of **the** heavens against men; for you do not enter, nor do you allow those that are entering to go in" (Mt. 23:13). *Note: Most translators choose to translate this phrase "the kingdom of heaven."*

12 ...ἐπλήσθησαν _____ ἡμέραι τοῦ τεκεῖν αὐτήν.

were fulfilled   the   days   (of) the   giving birth   of her

Entire verse: "It happened, while they were there, that **the** days were fulfilled that she should give birth" (Lk. 2:6).

13 ...τοῖς βαστάσασι τὸ βάρος _____ ἡμέρας...

those   having borne   the   burden   (of) the   day

Entire verse: "saying, 'These last have spent one hour, and you have made them equal to us, who have borne the burden of **the** day and the scorching heat!'" (Mt. 20:12)

14 δοκεῖτε ὅτι εἰρήνην παρεγενόμην δοῦναι ἐν _____ γῇ...

think you   that   peace   I came   to give   in   the   earth

Entire verse: "Do you think that I have come to give peace in **the** earth? I tell you, no, but rather division" (Lk. 12:51).

Exercise 6.1 – Choose the Article, *continued*

15 μακάριοι οἱ καθαροὶ ____ καρδίᾳ, ὅτι αὐτοὶ ____ Θεὸν ὄψονται.

    blessed   the   pure   (in) the   heart   for   they   (the)   God   will see

Entire verse: "Blessed are the pure in heart, for they shall see God" (Mt. 5:8). *Note that the definite article is removed from before both the word "heart" and the word "God" in English translation.*

16 ...Ὡσαννὰ ____ υἱῷ Δαυείδ...

    Hosanna   (to) the   son   of David

Entire verse: "The multitudes who went before him, and who followed kept shouting, "Hosanna to **the** son of David! Blessed is he who comes in the name of the Lord! Hosanna in the highest!" (Mt. 21:9)

17 ...Μὴ δύνανται ____ υἱοὶ τοῦ νυμφῶνος πενθεῖν...

    not   can   the   sons   of the   bridechamber   mourn

Entire verse: "And Jesus said to them, 'Can **the** sons of the bride-chamber mourn, so long as the bridegroom is with them? but days shall come when the bridegroom may be taken from them, and then they shall fast'" (Mt. 9:15).

18 ...καὶ ἡρπάσθη ____ τέκνον αὐτῆς πρὸς ____ Θεὸν...

    and   was caught up   the   child   of her   to   (the)   God

Entire verse: "She gave birth to a son, a male child, who is to rule all the nations with a rod of iron. **The** child of hers was caught up to God, and to his throne" (Rev. 12:5) *Note again the stripping of the article before the word "God" in English translation.*

19 Ἀρχὴ ____ εὐαγγελίου Ἰησοῦ Χριστοῦ Υἱοῦ Θεοῦ.

    beginning   (of) the   gospel   of Jesus   Christ   Son   of God

Entire verse: "The beginning of **the** Good News of Jesus Christ, the Son of God" (Mk. 1:1).

Answers: 15. τῇ (DFS), τὸν (AMS) 16. τῷ (DMS) 17. οἱ (NMP) 18. τὸ (NNS), τὸν (AMS) 19. τοῦ (GNS)

Exercise 6.1 – Choose the Article, *continued*

20 ...καὶ _____ πρόσωπα αὐτῶν ὡς πρόσωπα ἀνθρώπων.

    and   *the*   *faces*   *of them*   *like*   *faces*   *of men*

Entire verse: "The shapes of the locusts were like horses prepared for war. On their heads were something like golden crowns, and **the** faces of them were like men's faces" (Rev. 9:7).

21 ...καὶ κλινουσῶν _____ πρόσωπα εἰς _____ γῆν...

    and   *bowing*   *the*   *faces*   *to*   *the*   *ground*

Entire verse: "Becoming terrified, they bowed [**their**] faces down to **the** earth. They said to them, 'Why do you seek the living among the dead?'" (Lk. 24:5) *Note the English translation of "they bowed their faces" rather than the literal "they bowed the faces," in adherence to standard English convention.*

22 ...καὶ εὐφραίνοντο ἐν _____ ἔργοις τῶν χειρῶν αὐτῶν.

    and   *rejoiced*   *in*   *the*   *works*   *of the*   *hands*   *of them*

Entire verse: "They made a calf in those days, and brought a sacrifice to the idol, and rejoiced in **the** works of their hands" (Acts 7:41).

23 ...καὶ ἐδικαιώθη ἡ σοφία ἀπὸ _____ ἔργων αὐτῆς.

    but   *is justified*   *the*   *wisdom*   *by*   *the*   *deeds*   *of her*

Entire verse: "The Son of Man came eating and drinking, and they say, 'Behold, a gluttonous man and a drunkard, a friend of tax collectors and sinners!' But wisdom is justified by her works" (Mt. 11:19). *Note: Some manuscripts have* Καὶ ἐδικαιώθη ἡ σοφία ἀπὸ τῶν τέκνων αὐτῆς, *"but wisdom is justified by her children." Note also that the article in Greek is included before the word "wisdom," but it is left out of the English translation.*

Answers: 20. τὰ (NNP)   21. τὰ (ANP), τὴν (AFS)   22. τοῖς (DNP)   23. τῶν (GNP)

Lesson 7: The Third Declension

This will be the last lesson of this book, so give yourself a pat on the back. You deserve it for getting this far. This lesson is all about the third (and final) category of nouns: **nouns whose stems end in a consonant.**

Before we proceed, though, we need to show you a fantastic tool: the *lexical listing*.

The lexical listing

If you'll recall from Book 1, the term **lexical form** means "**the form of the word that is used in a dictionary (lexicon) listing.**" In Book 1, we explained that Greek dictionary editors arrived at a standard about what form they should use for the nouns in their dictionary entries. They certainly didn't want (or need) to list *every* form of *every* noun, so they had to pick the best one. (Dictionary editors will do anything in their power to reduce the size of the entries.) Anyhow, they all decided to use the **nominative singular form** as the **lexical form**. That's the form of the noun that you see when you look it up in a dictionary.

There are **two other pieces of information** that good Greek dictionaries or glossaries always provide, and they're usually listed directly *after* the entry word, which, as we said, is in the nominative singular form.

The **first** additional piece of information is **a partial spelling of the genitive singular form, showing only the last several letters**. Now, the editors usually don't list the *entire* genitive form, because they want to be brief and save space. Instead, they list the *minimum number of letters you need* to be able to recognize which spelling pattern the genitive form follows.

The **second** additional piece of information is the form of the **article** that agrees with the nominative singular form.

Why these two particular pieces of information? Without bogging you down with extra information right now, trust us that having the **genitive form memorized** will greatly serve you in your Greek studies. So, beginning now, **you should begin to memorize the genitive singular form right along with the nominative singular form.** As to memorizing the **article**, it is the key to remembering the noun's **gender**.

On the next page are a couple of typical dictionary entries illustrating how the lexical listing looks.

Examples of lexical listings

Here are some typical lexical listings. The first thing listed is the entry (in nominative singular form). Next are the minimum number of letters required to see which spelling the genitive singular form follows. After that is the article. Following all that is the definition.

ἄνθρωπος, -ου, ὁ a man, also the generic term for "mankind," one of the human race; people (including women and men).

βασιλεία, -ας, ἡ kingship, sovereignty, rule, kingdom, authority.

ἔργον, -ου, τό work, labor, action, deed, that which is wrought or made, that which is accomplished or intentionally carried out.

Ἰησοῦς, -οῦ, ὁ Jesus, Joshua (from Hebrew Yeshua/Yehoshua), meaning "the LORD saves" or "the LORD is salvation."

φωνή, -ῆς, ἡ a sound, noise, voice, language, dialect.

As we begin to study the forms of the third declension, you will soon reap the benefits of understanding how the lexical listing system works. It's a great shorthand system that helps us all remember what spelling pattern each noun should follow.

Accordion-like stems

Have you ever folded a piece of paper back and forth to make a paper fan? This is called an accordion fold, named after the folds of the bellows of an accordion.

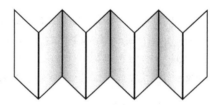

Up until now, we've dealt with first and second declension words whose stems seem fairly stable and unchanging. This makes it super easy to add case endings to them, and easy to discern the stems when you're looking at one of the forms. But, get ready for this. Certain third declension Greek nouns have stems which can shorten and lengthen in length. They'll shorten for certain cases (like the nominative, in which they seem to lose letters) and then lengthen for other cases (in which they seem to gain letters). We made up the term "accordion-like" for these stems.

Accordion-like stems in English

English doesn't have many stems which shorten and lengthen when you add different suffixes and prefixes, but it has a *few* words which at least have the appearance of doing so. We included these examples to help you understand this strange phenomenon in Greek nouns.

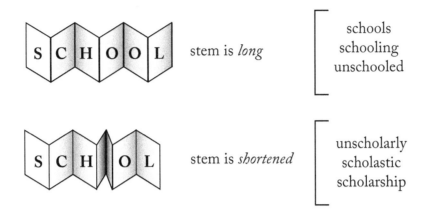

stem is *long*

[schools
schooling
unschooled]

stem is *shortened*

[unscholarly
scholastic
scholarship]

Notice that the shortened form looks as if it squeezed the extra O inside the narrowest fold to hide it from view. You can think of this as the extra O being *deleted*, too. Here's another:

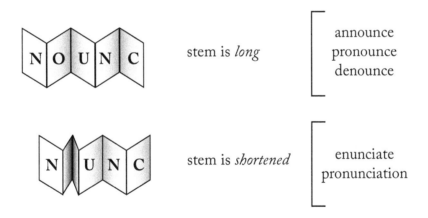

stem is *long*

[announce
pronounce
denounce]

stem is *shortened*

[enunciate
pronunciation]

And one more. In this one, the B gets hidden in the folds (or deleted, if you will).

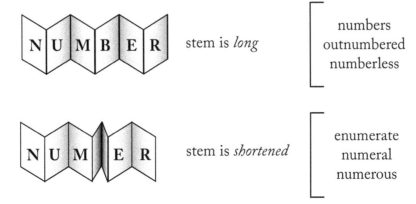

stem is *long*

[numbers
outnumbered
numberless]

stem is *shortened*

[enumerate
numeral
numerous]

Accordion-like stems in Greek third declension nouns

Let's look at an important third declension noun in Greek which you first learned in Book 1: ὄνομα. We'll begin with its lexical listing.

ὄνομα, -ματος, τό   name, character, fame, reputation

After reading the definition, what other information can we glean? We can tell from the **article** that the word is **neuter**. We can also see the **nominative singular** form and the **genitive singular ending letters**. Those genitive ending letters are very telling, because they inform us that the stem is accordion-like, as will soon become evident when you review the declension below. (This is one reason why you need to memorize the genitive singular form as well as the nominative singular form for every Greek noun, along with its gender.)

Now: Let's see how this noun, ὄνομα, declines.

nom sg	ὄνομα		*nom pl*	ὀνόματα
gen sg	ὀνόματος		*gen pl*	ὀνομάτων
dat sg	ὀνόματι		*dat pl*	ὀνόμασι(ν)
acc sg	ὄνομα		*acc pl*	ὀνόματα

Just by glancing at the spellings, you can see the accordion-like nature of this stem:

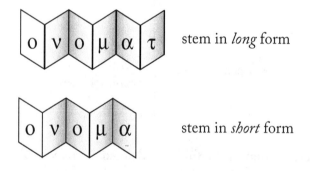

stem in *long* form

stem in *short* form

The cause of this shortening in the stem's length was **the deletion of the letter tau.** The reason this occurred is because of a rule that **there can never be a tau at the end of a Greek word.** In the nominative singular and accusative singular case forms for third declension neuter nouns, there are no added case ending letters, so, in this particular word, that final tau had to be lopped off. (We'll soon show you the paradigm for case endings; for now, we just want to illustrate accordion-like stems).

Another example of an accordion-like stem

Here's an important third declension noun in Greek: ἄρχων. We'll begin with its lexical listing.

ἄρχων, -οντος, ὁ   a preeminent ruler, chief, governor, leader; among the Jews, a member of the assembly of elders

We can tell from the **article** that the word is **masculine**. We can also see the **nominative singular** form and the **genitive singular ending letters**. The genitive ending letters let us know that this is another of those nouns with an accordion-like stem.

Now let's see how this noun, ἄρχων, declines.

nom sg	ἄρχων		*nom pl*	ἄρχοντες
gen sg	ἄρχοντος		*gen pl*	ἀρχόντων
dat sg	ἄρχοντι		*dat pl*	ἄρχουσι(ν)
acc sg	ἄρχοντα		*acc pl*	ἄρχοντας

Here are the two forms of the stem:

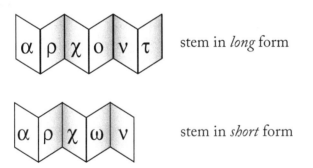

stem in *long* form

stem in *short* form

Did you notice in the short form of the stem that a vowel change occurred, as well as the loss of the tau? The omicron lengthened to an omega. **Vowel shortening and lengthening happens often**, so don't be alarmed if you ever see this.

Our more astute readers will have noticed some strange changes to the stem in the dative plural form, too. That happened because of another rule that says **certain letters drop out whenever they are followed by a sigma.** Yet another rule says **an extra vowel may be added to compensate for the loss of those letters**, which is the reason for the additional upsilon here. (Don't be concerned about these details now; we'll give you a list of all the spelling rules you'll need to know on the next pages.)

The movable nu

You may have noticed in these declensions a letter nu in parentheses (ν) at the very end of the dative plural case. Whenever a nu in parentheses appears in a paradigm, that's the signal that it's a movable nu. A **movable nu** is a nu which is **added to the end of a word if it precedes another word beginning with a vowel.** This prevents an awkward stopping of the voice between two vowel sounds; it makes speech more fluid. The movable nu is often used at the end of clauses or verses, too. If you think about it, you're already familiar with this phenomenon, because English has its own version of the movable nu. We attach an "n" to the indefinite article "a" when it precedes a word that begins with a vowel sound.

a cow   *When "a" is followed by a word beginning with a consonant, we don't add the "n"*
an ant   *When "a" is followed by a word beginning with a vowel, we add the "n"*

Stop consonants

Ready for more big-time terminology? Following are linguist's terms for the simple things we all do whenever we open our mouths to speak. Understanding how **stop consonants** change the spellings of third declension stems will save you *hours* of unnecessary paradigm memorization.

A **stop** is just a certain *type* of consonant. It's any consonant that is formed when we either **slow down** or **completely stop the flow of air** through the mouth. We do this with our lips *(labial)*, with the backs of our tongues against the soft part of the roof of our mouth *(velar or palatal)*, or by touching our tongues against the backs of our teeth *(dental)*. Examples in English:

Labial (lips):	P, B, PH (or F)
Velar (back of tongue to roof of mouth):	K, G, CH (as in Bach)
Dental (tongue to tooth):	T, D, TH

If we try to say these same sounds followed immediately by the "S" sound, they either create a new sound entirely, or become so awkward to pronounce that it's easier to just say "S".

Labial:	P+S = PS	B+S = BS	PH+S = PHS	*All sound very close to "PS"*
Velar:	K+S = KS	G+S = GS	CH+S = CHS	*All sound very close to "X"*
Dental:	T+S = TS	D+S = DS	TH+S = THS	*All sound very close to "S"*

Greek also has stop consonants. In fact, if you just replace the English letters from the examples above with the equivalent Greek letters, you'll see how Greek's stop consonants follow the same basic sound patterns. However, in Greek, the minute that one of these letter pairs comes into existence, it *immediately* gets replaced by a new, single letter which represents the new sound.

Labial:	$\pi+\sigma = \psi$	$\beta+\sigma = \psi$	$\phi+\sigma = \psi$	$\pi\sigma$, $\beta\sigma$ *and* $\phi\sigma$ *get replaced by* ψ *("PS")*
Velar:	$\kappa+\sigma = \xi$	$\gamma+\sigma = \xi$	$\chi+\sigma = \xi$	$\kappa\sigma$, $\gamma\sigma$ *and* $\chi\sigma$ *get replaced by* ξ *("X")*
Dental:	$\tau+\sigma = \sigma$	$\delta+\sigma = \sigma$	$\theta+\sigma = \sigma$	$\tau\sigma$, $\delta\sigma$ *and* $\theta\sigma$ *get replaced by* σ *("S")*

Spelling rules you need to know in order to proceed to learn third declension forms

There are spelling changes that tend to occur with certain Greek letter positions/combinations. Some of these were mentioned over the last several pages, but there are additional rules also listed here. **Please learn and memorize all these rules.**

A A **tau** will be **deleted** if it ever finds itself **at the very end of a word.**

B A **third declension stem consonant** may **change,** or even appear to **drop off,** when adding a **sigma** to it. Sometimes this is due to stop consonants (see discussion on prior page).

Labial stop consonant stem ending: $(\pi, \beta, \phi) + \sigma = \psi$
Velar stop consonant stem ending: $(\kappa, \gamma, \chi) + \sigma = \xi$
Dental stop consonant stem ending: $(\tau, \delta, \theta) + \sigma = \sigma$
Other stem endings: $\nu + \sigma = \sigma$ $\quad \nu\tau + \sigma = \sigma$

C A **movable nu** (indicated by nu in parentheses in paradigms) may be added when necessary, as when two adjacent vowel sounds would create an awkward stopping of the voice.

D An **iota** can only appear as a **subscript** under the letters **eta, omega** and **alpha**. It can't subscript underneath a consonant at all. So, in the dative case of third declension nouns where the case ending of iota ends up following a final stem *consonant*, the iota *can't* subscript and is forced to remain "full sized." It will stand next to the consonant on the same line.

Other spelling rules that are good to understand

Our paradigm charts don't show all the nitty gritty details of the processes that occur to make the forms, just the resulting changes. Below are some "behind the scenes" facts. It's good to comprehend these "background reasons" for case changes, because third declension nouns can have similar situations. This way, they won't seem so alien when you encounter them.

• The *true* genitive singular case ending in the second declension is omicron, not upsilon. However, when you add an omicron to a stem already ending in omicron, you get **two omicrons in a row.** There's a rule that the **second omicron** has to be changed to an **upsilon.** Example: $\lambda o \gamma o + o = \lambda ó \gamma o \upsilon$.

• The *true* accusative plural case ending is $\nu \varsigma$ in the first and second declensions. So, if you add this ending to a noun having a final stem vowel of omicron, the nu drops out, and an **additional vowel is added to compensate for this loss of a letter.** Example: $o + \nu \varsigma = o \upsilon \varsigma$.

• When adding a genitive plural case ending $\omega \nu$ to a stem vowel, the **omega swallows up the stem vowel.** Examples: $o + \omega \nu = \omega \nu$. $\quad \alpha + \omega \nu = \omega \nu$.

Is your head swirling? A word of encouragement

If your head isn't swirling from all the information that was dumped on you in the preceding pages, then you are an extraordinary student, indeed. You might not even be from this planet.

In our humble opinion, there seems to be an *inordinate* number of rules to know before embarking on the third declension. Believe us, if there were any easier way to introduce the third declension to you, we'd do it that way instead. But there isn't.

In fact, the first time we tried to understand all these rules, we had to re-read the chapter *seven different times* in the textbook we were using. We stuck post-it notes all over the chapter to make it easy to go back and find the rules, because every time we came across a third declension noun, we'd go, "*HUH?* What in the *world?*" And we'd have to turn back to that chapter to refresh our memories about what was going on with those strange stem changes.

So, if you're feeling lost in a fog, that's *completely normal.* If you've already gone ahead and stuck post-it notes all over the preceding pages, good for you! If you haven't, then please, join the rest of the human race, get out your highlighter and colored markers, and mark up the entire lesson with stars and arrows and circles and underlines. Cover it with post-it notes. Because that's what *we* had to do.

The good news is that you're about to see examples of these rules using real words. Real life examples always clarify and simplify everything. If you'll accompany us through the next several pages, quietly observing while we explain everything, you'll start to feel somewhat comfortable with the third declension.

Think about it. How did you ever get comfortable with all the outlandish rules of the English language? By gradual, repeated exposure. Greek will come to you in exactly the same way – by gradual, repeated exposure.

We're going to slowly and deliberately walk you through each and every example. We'll explain every single step. Will you promise to stay with us? Don't give up now! You're almost done with the entire book, after all. Just be patient with yourself. Let yourself learn at your own pace. If it takes you longer than you would like to learn this lesson, so what? So, it takes longer. If you keep making mistakes, so what? That's how we all learn. Trying and failing – making mistakes – is the *best* way to learn a language (or any other discipline).

And don't forget to ask for our Lord's intervention. He will supernaturally help you to get through this lesson on the third declension (just as He did for us), and *then* you will understand all three declensions of Greek nouns. *Sweet victory!*

The paradigm for the third declension

It's time to see the case endings of the third declension. We just tacked three more columns onto your good ol' paradigm of the first and second declensions. For your convenience, we included parentheses with the numbers (1), (2) or (3) in the column headers to indicate all the declensions. Recall the definitions of the three declensions: **First declension** nouns have stems ending in **alpha** or **eta** (and they are primarily feminine, with some exceptions). **Second declension** nouns have stems ending in **omicron** (and they are mostly masculine or neuter, with some exceptions). **Third declension** nouns are any nouns with stems ending in a **consonant** (and they can be any gender).

The paradigm for all noun case endings

Letter shaded in gray means that the final stem vowel changes to that vowel.
Any nu enclosed in parentheses is a movable nu.
Notice that the masculine and feminine columns of the third declension are completely identical.

	First & Second Declensions			Third Declension		
	masc (2)	fem (1)	neut (2)	masc (3)	fem (3)	neut (3)
nom sg	ς	–	ν	ς	ς	–
gen sg	υ	ς	υ	ος	ος	ος
dat sg	ι*	ι*	ι*	ι	ι	ι
acc sg	ν	ν	ν	α/ν**	α/ν**	–

	masc (2)	fem (1)	neut (2)	masc (3)	fem (3)	neut (3)
nom pl	ι	ι	α	ες	ες	α
gen pl	ων	ων	ων	ων	ων	ων
dat pl	ις	ις	ις	σι(ν)	σι(ν)	σι(ν)
acc pl	υς	ς	α	ας	ας	α

* In the dative singular case of the first and second declensions, the final stem vowel *lengthens* and the iota *subscripts*. (This can't happen in the third declension, because third declension stems end in a consonant, so the iota has to stay on the line.)

** The reason for the slash between the two letters is because sometimes the case ending will be alpha, sometimes nu.

First example of a third declension noun: σάρξ

Let's begin with an important noun to know: σάρξ. It's always good to start with the lexical listing.

σάρξ, σαρκός, ἡ   flesh, body (*In scripture, positive and negative connotations include:* materiality/physicality, that which is carnal, physically-related kindred, of human nature, of human origin, of human empowerment unaided by God, that which is thought or done apart from God's inner spiritual working)

First of all, notice by the article that we are dealing with a *feminine* noun. Next, if we look at the spelling of the genitive form, we can see that the long form of the stem includes the letter kappa. Somehow, in the short form of the stem (which we can see in the nominative case), the letter kappa either *disappeared* or got *changed*. We'll be able to tell what happened there as soon as we study the declension of this noun.

Here's how this noun declines. For your convenience, we also clipped a piece of the paradigm from the previous page (just the third declension endings) and pasted it below at left. We highlighted in gray the column that applies to this particular noun – the *feminine* column.

Third Declension		
masc (3)	fem (3)	neut (3)
nom sg ς	ς	–
gen sg ος	ος	ος
dat sg ι	ι	ι
acc sg α/ν	α/ν	–

nom pl ες	ες	α
gen pl ων	ων	ων
dat pl σι(ν)	σι(ν)	σι(ν)
acc pl ας	ας	α

Declension of σάρξ

nom sg	σάρξ
gen sg	σαρκός
dat sg	σαρκί
acc sg	σάρκα
nom pl	σάρκες
gen pl	σαρκῶν
dat pl	σαρξί(ν)
acc pl	σάρκας

In the **genitive** case spelling (which includes the "long" form of the stem), **we can still see the letter kappa**. This means kappa must be part of the **original stem**, σαρκ, and it must have gotten removed or changed in the nominative form. Now that you know the *true* stem spelling, σαρκ, read how each case form was created, below. (You'll also need to refer to your Rules on page 89.)

nom sg	σάρξ	The case ending of ς was applied to the stem σαρκ. This resulted in σαρκς. The letter combination of κς was instantly replaced by the letter ξ, because of Rule B.
gen sg	σαρκός	The case ending of ος was applied to the stem σαρκ.
dat sg	σαρκί	The case ending of ι was applied to the stem σαρκ. The iota would ordinarily try to subscript in the dative singular case, but it can't, because kappa is not a vowel.
acc sg	σάρκα	The case ending of α was applied to the stem σαρκ. This alpha is different from 1st & 2nd declension nouns. It truly is a case ending unto itself, rather than a changed stem vowel.
nom pl	σάρκες	The case ending of ες was applied to the stem σαρκ.
gen pl	σαρκῶν	The case ending of ων was applied to the stem σαρκ. The genitive plural is very nice – its case ending is completely consistent in any declension – 1st, 2nd or 3rd.
dat pl	σαρξί(ν)	The case ending of σι was applied to the stem σαρκ. This resulted in σαρκσι. The letter combination of κσ was instantly replaced by the letter ξ, again because of Rule B. The movable nu is also included here (Rule C).
acc pl	σάρκας	The case ending of ας was applied to the stem σαρκ. Notice that *this* alpha is actually part of the case ending. Try not to confuse *this* ending, ας, with that of gen. sg. or acc. pl. forms of first declension nouns whose *stems* happen to end in alpha.

Second example of a third declension noun: ὄνομα

Here's a noun you learned way back in Book 1: ὄνομα.

ὄνομα, -ματος, τό   name, reputation, character, fame (a manifestation of one's character that makes him distinct from others; i.e., a name is an expression of one's very essence, according to Hebraic thought)

First, look at the article. From this, we see that we are dealing with a *neuter* noun. Next, look at the spelling of the genitive form. In this lexical listing, we can only see its last several letters, but that's certainly enough to tell us that the long form of the stem includes the letter tau. This is one clue that we're not dealing with a stem ending in alpha. Therefore, we're dealing with a third declension noun, for sure.

Here's how this noun declines. In your paradigm, we highlighted in gray the column that applies to this particular noun – the *neuter* column.

	Third Declension		
	masc (3)	fem (3)	neut (3)
nom sg	ς	ς	–
gen sg	ος	ος	ος
dat sg	ι	ι	ι
acc sg	α/ν	α/ν	–
nom pl	ες	ες	α
gen pl	ων	ων	ων
dat pl	σι(ν)	σι(ν)	σι(ν)
acc pl	ας	ας	α

Declension of ὄνομα

nom sg	ὄνομα
gen sg	ὀνόματος
dat sg	ὀνόματι
acc sg	ὄνομα
nom pl	ὀνόματα
gen pl	ὀνομάτων
dat pl	ὀνόμασι(ν)
acc pl	ὀνόματα

In the **genitive** case spelling (which includes the "long" form of the stem), **we can still see the letter tau**. This means tau must be part of the **original stem**: ονοματ.   That stem somehow got shortened (or changed) in the nominative case.   Let's find out.

nom sg	ὄνομα	There is no case ending to apply to the stem ονοματ in the nominative singular case. This results in a word spelled ονοματ, which then needs to have the tau deleted because of Rule A – no tau allowed at the end of a word. The stem essentially gets "cut back" to a shortened form.
gen sg	ὀνόματος	The case ending of ος was applied to the stem ονοματ.
dat sg	ὀνόματι	The case ending of ι was applied to the stem ονοματ. The iota would ordinarily try to subscript in the dative singular case, but it can't, because tau is not a vowel.
acc sg	ὄνομα	This form is a duplicate of the nominative singular form, because both have the same case endings. In fact, all neuter nouns have identical forms for nominative & accusative.
nom pl	ὀνόματα	The case ending of α was applied to the stem ονοματ. This results in a nicely differentiated form from the nominative singular. The nominative *plural* has the *entire, long-form* stem; the nominative *singular* has the *shortened* stem.
gen pl	ὀνομάτων	The case ending of ων was applied to the stem ονοματ.
dat pl	ὀνόμασι(ν)	The case ending of σι was applied to the stem ονοματ. This resulted in ονοματσι. The letter combination of τσ was instantly replaced by just the letter σ, because of Rule B. The movable nu is also included here (Rule C).
acc pl	ὀνόματα	The case ending of α was applied to the stem ονοματ. This form is a duplicate of the nominative plural form. All neuter nouns have identical forms for nominative & accusative.

Third example of a third declension noun: ἐλπίς

Here's a great word for you to know.

ἐλπίς, -ίδος, ἡ   hope, expectation of what is certain, trust, anticipation, confidence.

The article tells us this is a *feminine* noun. The ending letters of the genitive case display a clear difference from the nominative case form, alerting us to the fact of an accordion-like stem. We can fully expect there to be differences in the stem's spelling throughout the declension.

Here's how this noun declines. In your paradigm, we highlighted the column in gray that applies to this particular noun – the *feminine* column.

Third Declension	masc (3)	fem (3)	neut (3)
nom sg	ς	ς	–
gen sg	ος	ος	ος
dat sg	ι	ι	ι
acc sg	α/ν	α/ν	–
nom pl	ες	ες	α
gen pl	ων	ων	ων
dat pl	σι(ν)	σι(ν)	σι(ν)
acc pl	ας	ας	α

Declension of ἐλπίς

nom sg	ἐλπίς
gen sg	ἐλπίδος
dat sg	ἐλπίδι
acc sg	ἐλπίδα
nom pl	ἐλπίδες
gen pl	ἐλπίδων
dat pl	ἐλπίσι(ν)
acc pl	ἐλπίδας

In the **genitive** case spelling we can catch a glimpse of the **original stem**, ελπιδ. Here's how it changed from one case to the next.

nom sg	ἐλπίς	The case ending of ς was applied to the stem ελπιδ. This resulted in ελπιδς. The letter combination of δς was instantly replaced by the letter ς, because of Rule B.
gen sg	ἐλπίδος	The case ending of ος was applied to the stem ελπιδ.
dat sg	ἐλπίδι	The case ending of ι was applied to the stem ελπιδ. The added iota would ordinarily try to subscript in the dative singular case, but it can't, because delta is not a vowel.
acc sg	ἐλπίδα	The case ending of α was applied to the stem ελπιδ.
nom pl	ἐλπίδες	The case ending of ες was applied to the stem ελπιδ.
gen pl	ἐλπίδων	The case ending of ων was applied to the stem ελπιδ.
dat pl	ἐλπίσι(ν)	The case ending of σι was applied to the stem ελπιδ. This resulted in ελπιδσι. The letter combination of δσ was instantly replaced by just the letter σ, because of Rule B. The movable nu is also included here (Rule C).
acc pl	ἐλπίδας	The case ending of ας was applied to the stem ελπιδ.

The *point* is... that you get the gist

We want to reassure you that you do **NOT** have to be worried about producing these forms yourself. It's way, way too early for that. Also, you do **NOT** have to be worried about memorizing any patterns you may have noticed in these third declension nouns. The reason we say this is because there are *so many variations* of third declension patterns that they will constantly surprise you. It would be unreasonable to ask anyone to learn them all by heart at this stage (or perhaps at *any* stage). A thin, introductory workbook like this one would never dream of attempting to describe all the possible pattern variations there are among third declension nouns. (As a matter of fact, if you're dying to see one such variation right now, go back to page 87, in which the word ἄρχων in the nominative singular form doesn't seem to follow the patterns we just taught in the last three examples, yet its other forms seem to adhere perfectly!)

Well, if *that's* the case, then *what* has been the point of this entire lesson?

The whole "point" of this lesson is really two-fold.

> 1. For you to get the "gist" of how third-declension stems might act like accordions (and a few of the reasons why they might do that).
>
> 2. For you to learn how to discern from the genitive spelling in a lexical listing if you might be dealing with an accordion-like stem. This will help you avoid confusing any *third* declension nouns (and all of their case endings) with *first* and *second* declension nouns (and all of *their* case endings).

If you've come away from this lesson feeling like, "Yeah. I think I've learned how to be aware of those two things," then we believe you have been successful in getting the "gist" of third declension nouns. That's all anyone could ever hope for at this stage.

How do you study scripture without knowing *all* the third declension patterns?

People who want to know *all* the patterns of *all* the nouns usually want this knowledge so that they can know the grammatical information of the noun, and thereby understand scripture better. That goal is admirable and wonderful. This should be *everyone's* motivation for learning Biblical Greek. However, it takes a long time to get to the point where you have all those variations of the patterns under your belt. Most of us *never* arrive. What to do in the meantime?

We ourselves are certainly no experts in Biblical Greek, let alone the many patterns of third declension nouns. We lean heavily on reference tools when we try to understand the New Testament. One book we use constantly is the *Analytical Greek New Testament* (Ed. Friberg, Friberg & Aland, Baker Publishing Group). This is just a Greek New Testament (no English translation), but underneath every single Greek word is a set of abbreviations giving you its grammar data (like its gender, case, etc.). We love it and cannot live without it.

Sometimes we prefer to use electronic tools instead. One of our favorite websites to visit is biblehub.com. The Greek portions of that site provide all the grammar data of every Greek word of the New Testament. It saves time, especially when we need to quickly see all the forms of a Greek word and the places it appears throughout the New Testament. As of the date of this book's publishing, biblehub.com is free for anyone to use, no sign-up or log-in required.

If you really want to buy your own software, there are many excellent programs out there. Just make sure that whatever software you buy contains the actual grammatical information of every Greek word. Choose one that is able to search on the Greek stems, not just English words.

One last thing about third declension nouns: Stems that end in consonantal iota

Before we leave you, we'd be remiss if we didn't inform you about a class of third declension nouns which *appear* to have a final stem vowel (iota). This is surprising, because the definition of "third declension" is when stems end in a consonant, right? Right! But, *this* iota is *special*.

Once upon a time, many years before the New Testament was written, there was special iota that was pronounced as a consonant, called the "consonantal iota." It sounded something like our "y" does whenever our "y" is used as a consonant. Over time, it fell out of use and ended up replaced by a "regular" iota (the one you're familiar with), or sometimes an epsilon.

Nowadays, you'll see an iota (or epsilon) mysteriously lurking at the end of certain noun stems where a consonant really ought to be. It looks and sounds like a harmless vowel. Deep in its little heart, though, it still thinks of itself as a consonant, and it still acts like one in certain ways (like the way it accepts the case endings). So, whenever an iota or epsilon is the final letter in third declension stems, don't let it fool you with its "Why, I'm just a sweet little ol' vowel" routine. Try to remember that it's going to have a "consonantal attitude" and will certainly act like it.

Here is an example of a third declension noun with a consonantal iota stem. This particular noun is very important to know, because it is used frequently in the New Testament.

πίστις, -εως, ἡ   faith, belief, trust, confidence; fidelity, faithfulness.

nom sg	πίστις
gen sg	πίστεως
dat sg	πίστει
acc sg	πίστιν
nom pl	πίστεις
gen pl	πίστεων
dat pl	πίστεσι(ν)
acc pl	πίστεις

You did it!

You finished Lesson 7! Can you believe it? *We* can. We knew you could do it, because *you can do all things through Christ who strengthens you.*

This book ends with some helpful tools.

First, there are some easy exercises to let you see third declension nouns in New Testament scripture. They begin on the next page. Being scripture, they will refresh your spirit after all that technical stuff you've had to wade through. You'll finally get rewarded for all your hard work with the third declension.

Next, we're including brand new vocabulary flashcards for you. They contain all the words you've learned so far in Books 1 and 2. Cut these new ones out and put your old cards aside, because these babies are an *upgrade*. They have a *lot* more information on them. They're like having a true lexical listing all on one card, plus a little more. These cards will make it easy for you to memorize the genitive case form along with the nominative case form and the definite article.

Finally, you'll find the glossary. All your words are in true lexical listing format, in alphabetical order.

One particular sixties cover band is always a big hit on the Greek festival circuit.

Exercise 7.1 – Scripture Match Up

Fill in the blanks of actual scripture below using the correct form of each third declension noun. Some of these words are from your top twenty nouns list. Some are more unfamiliar to you. To make the exercise as easy as possible, we included a word bank at the top of every page which lists and defines all the case forms of the noun. All you have to do is copy the correct form into the blank. If there happens to be a definite article that precedes the blank, take the time to analyze it. The article will always provide your *best* hint to figure out the noun's case form, because the article *has* to agree with the noun.

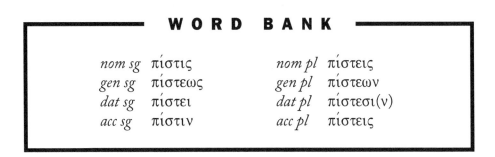

```
W O R D   B A N K

nom sg  πίστις          nom pl  πίστεις
gen sg  πίστεως         gen pl  πίστεων
dat sg  πίστει          dat pl  πίστεσι(ν)
acc sg  πίστιν          acc pl  πίστεις
```

❶ ...ἤνοιξεν   τοῖς   ἔθνεσιν   θύραν   _____.

    he opened   to the   Gentiles   a door   of faith

Entire verse: "When they had arrived, and had gathered the assembly together, they reported all the things that God had done with them, and that he had opened a door of **faith** to the nations" (Acts 14:27).

❷ ἄρα   ἡ   _____   ἐξ   ἀκοῆς...

    so   [the]   faith   by   hearing

Entire verse: "So **faith** comes by hearing, and hearing by the word of God" (Rom. 10:17).

❸ ...ἐὰν   ἔχητε   _____   ὡς   κόκκον   σινάπεως...

    if   you have   faith   as   a seed   of mustard

Entire verse: "He said to them, 'Because of your unbelief. For most certainly I tell you, if you have **faith** as a grain of mustard seed, you will tell this mountain, "Move from here to there," and it will move; and nothing will be impossible for you'" (Mt. 17:20).

Answers: 1. πίστεως (GFS)   2. πίστις (NFS)   3. πίστιν (AFS)

Exercise 7.1 – Scripture Match Up, *continued*

```
┌──────────────────── W O R D   B A N K ────────────────────┐
│                                                            │
│     nom sg  ἀνήρ          nom pl  ἄνδρες                    │
│     gen sg  ἀνδρός        gen pl  ἀνδρῶν                    │
│     dat sg  ἀνδρί         dat pl  ἀνδράσι(ν)                │
│     acc sg  ἄνδρα         acc pl  ἄνδρας                    │
│                                                            │
└────────────────────────────────────────────────────────────┘
```

4 παραγενόμενοι   δὲ   πρὸς   αὐτὸν   οἱ _____ εἶπαν...

having come   *moreover*   *to*   *him*   *the*   *men*   *said*

Entire verse: "Having come to him, the **men** said, 'John the Baptizer has sent us to you, saying, "Are you he who comes, or should we look for another?"'" (Luke 7:20)

5 ...σύρων   τε   _____   καὶ   γυναῖκας...

dragging off *moreover*   *men*   *and*   *women*

Entire verse: "But Saul ravaged the assembly, entering into every house, and dragged both **men** and women off to prison" (Acts 8:3).

6 Ἰακὼβ   δὲ   ἐγέννησεν   τὸν   Ἰωσὴφ   τὸν   _____   Μαρίας...

Jacob   *moreover*   *begat*   *-*   *Joseph*   *the*   *husband*   *of Mary*

Entire verse: "Jacob begat Joseph, the **husband** of Mary, from whom was born Jesus, who is called Christ" (Mt. 1:16).

7 ...καὶ   εἰσήλθομεν   εἰς   τὸν   οἶκον   τοῦ   _____

and   *we entered*   *into*   *the*   *house*   *of the*   *man*

Entire verse: "The Spirit told me to go with them, without discriminating. These six brothers also accompanied me, and we entered into the **man's** house" (Acts 11:12).

Answers: 4. ἄνδρες (NMP)   5. ἄνδρας (AMP)   6. ἄνδρα (AMS)   7. ἀνδρός (GMS)

──── W O R D   B A N K ────

nom sg	χάρις	*nom pl*	χάριτες
gen sg	χάριτος	*gen pl*	χαρίτων
dat sg	χάριτι	*dat pl*	χάρισι(ν)
acc sg	χάριν	*acc pl*	χάριτας

8 ...εὗρες   γὰρ   _____   παρὰ   τῷ   Θεῷ.

   you have found   indeed   favor   with   –   God

Entire verse: "The angel said to her, 'Don't be afraid, Mary, for you have found **favor** with God'" (Luke 1:30).

9 ...καλέσαντος   ὑμᾶς   ἐν   _____   Χριστοῦ...

   having called   you   in   grace   of Christ

Entire verse: "I marvel that you are so quickly deserting him who called you in the **grace** of Christ to a different gospel..." (Gal. 1:6)

10 ..._____   τε   μεγάλη   ἦν   ἐπὶ   πάντας   αὐτούς.

   grace   moreover   abundant   was   upon   all   them

Entire verse: "With great power, the apostles gave their testimony of the resurrection of the Lord Jesus. Great **grace** was on them all" (Acts 4:33).

11 προσερχώμεθα   οὖν   μετὰ   παρρησίας   τῷ   θρόνῳ   τῆς   _____

   we should come   therefore   with   boldness   to the   throne   of grace

Entire verse: "Let us therefore draw near with boldness to the throne of **grace**, that we may receive mercy, and may find grace for help in time of need" (Heb. 4:16).

Answers: 8. χάριν (AFS)   9. χάριτι (DFS)   10. χάρις (NFS)   11. χάριτος (GFS)

Exercise 7.1 – Scripture Match Up, *continued*

W O R D   B A N K

nom sg	πνεῦμα	*nom pl*	πνεύματα
gen sg	πνεύματος	*gen pl*	πνευμάτων
dat sg	πνεύματι	*dat pl*	πνεύμασι(ν)
acc sg	πνεῦμα	*acc pl*	πνεύματα

12 ...καὶ ὁ Κύριος ὁ Θεὸς τῶν _____ τῶν προφητῶν...

and   the   Lord   the   God   of the   spirits   of the   prophets

Entire verse: "He said to me, 'These words are faithful and true. The Lord God of the **spirits** of the prophets sent his angel to show to his bondservants the things which must happen soon'" (Rev. 22:6).

13 αὐτὸς ὑμᾶς βαπτίσει ἐν _____ ἁγίῳ καὶ πυρί...

he   you   will baptize   in   spirit   holy   and   [in] fire

Entire verse: "I indeed baptize you in water for repentance, but he who comes after me is mightier than I, whose shoes I am not worthy to carry. He will baptize you in the Holy **Spirit** and in fire" (Mt. 3:11).

14 ...καὶ ἐξέβαλεν τὰ _____ λόγῳ...

and   he cast out   the   spirits   [by] a word

Entire verse: "When evening came, they brought to him many possessed with demons. He cast out the **spirits** with a word, and healed all who were sick..." (Mt. 8:16)

15 ...καὶ τοῖς _____ τοῖς ἀκαθάρτοις ἐπιτάσσει...

even   the   spirits   -   unclean   he commands

Entire verse: "They were all amazed, so that they questioned among themselves, saying, 'What is this? A new teaching? For with authority he commands even the unclean **spirits**, and they obey him!'" (Mk. 1:27) *Hint: The direct object ("an order" or "a command") is not explicitly spelled out here. He commands "a command" to the spirits. "Spirits" is therefore the indirect object. The definite article further verifies that this is the case.*

Answers: 12. πνευμάτων (GNP) 13. πνεύματι (DNS) 14. πνεύματα (ANP) 15. πνεύμασι (DNP)

Exercise 7.1 – Scripture Match Up, *continued*

WORD BANK

nom sg	πατήρ	*nom pl*	πατέρες
gen sg	πατρός	*gen pl*	πατέρων
dat sg	πατρί	*dat pl*	πατράσι(ν)
acc sg	πατέρα	*acc pl*	πατέρας

16 εἶπεν δὲ ὁ _____ πρὸς τοὺς δούλους αὐτοῦ...

said   moreover   the   father   to   the   servants   of him

Entire verse: "But the **father** said to his servants, 'Bring out the best robe, and put it on him. Put a ring on his hand, and shoes on his feet'" (Lk. 15:22).

17 ...οἱ _____ ἐκοιμήθησαν...

the   fathers   fell asleep

Entire verse: "and saying, 'Where is the promise of his coming? For, from the day that the **fathers** fell asleep, all things continue as they were from the beginning of the creation'" (2 Pet. 3:4).

18 Ὁ φιλῶν _____ ἢ μητέρα ὑπὲρ ἐμὲ οὐκ ἔστιν μου ἄξιος...

the   loving   father   or   mother   above   me   not   is   of me   worthy
[one]

Entire verse: "He who loves **father** or mother more than me is not worthy of me; and he who loves son or daughter more than me isn't worthy of me" (Mt. 10:37).

19 οὐ κατὰ τὴν διαθήκην ἣν ἐποίησα τοῖς _____ αὐτῶν...

not according to the covenant that I made [with] the fathers   of them

Entire verse: "'not according to the covenant that I made with their **fathers**, in the day that I took them by the hand to lead them out of the land of Egypt; for they didn't continue in my covenant, and I disregarded them,' says the Lord" (Heb. 8:9).   *Hint: This particular case form, at least in this particular verse, does make use of the movable nu.*

Answers: 16. πατήρ (NMS)   17. πατέρες (NMP)   18. πατέρα (AMS)   19. πατράσιν (DMP)

Greek students have some of the worst nightmares.

Complete Flashcard Set
For Vocabulary of Books 1 and 2

These pages contain all the words introduced in Books 1 and 2 of this series, in alphabetical order. This set of cards supersedes prior sets, because it contains the lexical listing and all the case forms. **Memorize each noun's gender and its nominative and genitive singular forms.**

ἀδελφός, –οῦ, ὁ

masculine noun, second declension

nom sg	ἀδελφός	nom pl	ἀδελφοί
gen sg	ἀδελφοῦ	gen pl	ἀδελφῶν
dat sg	ἀδελφῷ	dat pl	ἀδελφοῖς
acc sg	ἀδελφόν	acc pl	ἀδελφούς
voc sg	ἀδελφέ / ἄδελφε	voc pl	ἀδελφοί

ἁμαρτία, –ας, ἡ

feminine noun, first declension

nom sg	ἁμαρτία	nom pl	ἁμαρτίαι
gen sg	ἁμαρτίας	gen pl	ἁμαρτιῶν
dat sg	ἁμαρτίᾳ	dat pl	ἁμαρτίαις
acc sg	ἁμαρτίαν	acc pl	ἁμαρτίας
voc sg	ἁμαρτία	voc pl	ἁμαρτίαι

ἀνήρ, ἀνδρός, ὁ

masculine noun, third declension

nom sg	ἀνήρ	nom pl	ἄνδρες
gen sg	ἀνδρός	gen pl	ἀνδρῶν
dat sg	ἀνδρί	dat pl	ἀνδράσι(ν)
acc sg	ἄνδρα	acc pl	ἄνδρας
voc sg	ἄνερ	voc pl	ἄνδρες

ἄνθρωπος, –ου, ὁ

masculine noun, second declension

nom sg	ἄνθρωπος	nom pl	ἄνθρωποι
gen sg	ἀνθρώπου	gen pl	ἀνθρώπων
dat sg	ἀνθρώπῳ	dat pl	ἀνθρώποις
acc sg	ἄνθρωπον	acc pl	ἀνθρώπους
voc sg	ἄνθρωπε	voc pl	ἄνθρωποι

ἄρχων, –οντος, ὁ

masculine noun, third declension

nom sg	ἄρχων	nom pl	ἄρχοντες
gen sg	ἄρχοντος	gen pl	ἀρχόντων
dat sg	ἄρχοντι	dat pl	ἄρχουσι(ν)
acc sg	ἄρχοντα	acc pl	ἄρχοντας
voc sg	ἄρχων / ἄρχον	voc pl	ἄρχοντες

βασιλεία, –ας, ἡ

feminine noun, first declension

nom sg	βασιλεία	nom pl	βασιλεῖαι
gen sg	βασιλείας	gen pl	βασιλειῶν
dat sg	βασιλείᾳ	dat pl	βασιλείαις
acc sg	βασιλείαν	acc pl	βασιλείας
voc sg	βασιλεία	voc pl	βασιλεῖαι

γῆ, γῆς, ἡ

feminine noun, first declension

nom sg	γῆ	nom pl	unused
gen sg	γῆς	gen pl	unused
dat sg	γῇ	dat pl	unused
acc sg	γῆν	acc pl	unused
voc sg	γῆ	voc pl	unused

γυνή, γυναικός, ἡ

feminine noun, third declension

nom sg	γυνή	nom pl	γυναῖκες
gen sg	γυναικός	gen pl	γυναικῶν
dat sg	γυναικί	dat pl	γυναιξί(ν)
acc sg	γυναῖκα	acc pl	γυναῖκας
voc sg	γύναι	voc pl	γυναῖκες

sin, moral failure/offense, ethical fault,
sinful deed or thought

Word origin: from the root of ἁμαρτάνω
"to miss, to fail"

(This card is from the final flashcard set of Book 2)

---

brother; *figuratively*, a member of the same
religious community (fellow believer)

Word origin: α + δελφύς *(womb),*
"one/same womb"

(This card is from the final flashcard set of Book 2)

---

man (male), mankind (male and female),
humanity, human being, person

Word origin uncertain, possibly from ἀνήρ

(This card is from the final flashcard set of Book 2)

---

man (adult male human being), husband

Word origin: a primary word

(This card is from the final flashcard set of Book 2)

---

kingdom, dominion, sovereignty, rule,
kingly authority. Esp. of God, both
concretely and in the hearts of men.

Word origin: from the stem of βασιλεύς, *"king"*

(This card is from the final flashcard set of Book 2)

---

ruler, prince, leader, chief. (Within first-
century Judaism, an official member of the
assembly of elders.)

Word origin: from the present participle of ἄρχω,
"to rule, take precedence, begin, start"

(This card is from the final flashcard set of Book 2)

---

woman, wife

Word origin: a primary word

(This card is from the final flashcard set of Book 2)

---

earth, soil/arable land, mainland, region
(i.e., a territory and its inhabitants)

Word origin: a primary word

(This card is from the final flashcard set of Book 2)

ἐλπίς, -ίδος, ἡ

feminine noun, third declension

nom sg	ἐλπίς	*nom pl*	ἐλπίδες
gen sg	ἐλπίδος	*gen pl*	ἐλπίδων
dat sg	ἐλπίδι	*dat pl*	ἐλπίσι(ν)
acc sg	ἐλπίδα	*acc pl*	ἐλπίδας
voc sg	*unused*	*voc pl*	*unused*

ἔργον, -ου, τό

neuter noun, second declension

nom sg	ἔργον	*nom pl*	ἔργα
gen sg	ἔργου	*gen pl*	ἔργων
dat sg	ἔργῳ	*dat pl*	ἔργοις
acc sg	ἔργον	*acc pl*	ἔργα
voc sg	ἔργον	*voc pl*	ἔργα

εὐαγγέλιον, -ου, τό

neuter noun, second declension

nom sg	εὐαγγέλιον	*nom pl*	εὐαγγέλια
gen sg	εὐαγγελίου	*gen pl*	εὐαγγελίων
dat sg	εὐαγγελίῳ	*dat pl*	εὐαγγελίοις
acc sg	εὐαγγέλιον	*acc pl*	εὐαγγέλια
voc sg	εὐαγγέλιον	*voc pl*	εὐαγγέλια

ζωή, -ῆς, ἡ

feminine noun, first declension

nom sg	ζωή	*nom pl*	*unused*
gen sg	ζωῆς	*gen pl*	*unused*
dat sg	ζωῇ	*dat pl*	*unused*
acc sg	ζωήν	*acc pl*	*unused*
voc sg	ζωή	*voc pl*	*unused*

ἡμέρα, -ας, ἡ

feminine noun, first declension

nom sg	ἡμέρα	*nom pl*	ἡμέραι
gen sg	ἡμέρας	*gen pl*	ἡμερῶν
dat sg	ἡμέρᾳ	*dat pl*	ἡμέραις
acc sg	ἡμέραν	*acc pl*	ἡμέρας
voc sg	ἡμέρα	*voc pl*	ἡμέραι

θεός, -οῦ, ὁ

masculine noun, second declension

nom sg	θεός	*nom pl*	θεοί
gen sg	θεοῦ	*gen pl*	θεῶν
dat sg	θεῷ	*dat pl*	θεοῖς
acc sg	θεόν	*acc pl*	θεούς
voc sg	θεέ	*voc pl*	θεοί

ἱερόν, -οῦ, τό

neuter noun, second declension

nom sg	ἱερόν	*nom pl*	ἱερά
gen sg	ἱεροῦ	*gen pl*	ἱερῶν
dat sg	ἱερῷ	*dat pl*	ἱεροῖς
acc sg	ἱερόν	*acc pl*	ἱερά
voc sg	ἱερόν	*voc pl*	ἱερά

Ἰησοῦς, -οῦ, ὁ

masculine proper noun

nom sg	Ἰησοῦς	*nom pl*	*unused*
gen sg	Ἰησοῦ	*gen pl*	*unused*
dat sg	Ἰησοῦ	*dat pl*	*unused*
acc sg	Ἰησοῦν	*acc pl*	*unused*
voc sg	Ἰησοῦ	*voc pl*	*unused*

καρδία, -ας, ἡ

feminine noun, first declension

nom sg	καρδία	*nom pl*	καρδίαι
gen sg	καρδίας	*gen pl*	καρδιῶν
dat sg	καρδίᾳ	*dat pl*	καρδίαις
acc sg	καρδίαν	*acc pl*	καρδίας
voc sg	καρδία	*voc pl*	καρδίαι

κόσμος, -ου, ὁ

masculine noun, second declension

nom sg	κόσμος	*nom pl*	κόσμοι
gen sg	κόσμου	*gen pl*	κόσμων
dat sg	κόσμῳ	*dat pl*	κόσμοις
acc sg	κόσμον	*acc pl*	κόσμους
voc sg	κόσμε	*voc pl*	κόσμοι

work, labor, action, deed, that which is wrought or made, something accomplished which carries out an intention or purpose

Word origin: from a primary (obsolete) verb "to work"

(This card is from the final flashcard set of Book 2)

hope, expectation, trust, confidence (in the certainty of that which is to come)

Word origin: from the same as ἐλπίζω "to hope with anticipation or expectation"

(This card is from the final flashcard set of Book 2)

life (spiritual or physical)

Word origin: from ζῶ, "to live"

(This card is from the final flashcard set of Book 2)

good news, the gospel; specifically, the glad tidings of the kingdom of God throughout Old and New Testaments

Word origin: from same as εὐαγγελίζω, from εὖ "good, well" + ἄγγελος "angel, messenger"; i.e., "good message"

(This card is from the final flashcard set of Book 2)

God, a god

Word origin uncertain

(This card is from the final flashcard set of Book 2)

day (daylight, as contrasted with night); or the civil day (in Judaism, the 24 hours beginning at sunset and concluding with the following sunset); or that prophesied "Day" in which the Lord shall judge men

Word origin: a primary word

(This card is from the final flashcard set of Book 2)

Jesus, i.e. Joshua (Hebrew, *Yeshua*, a short form of the Hebrew name *Yehoshua*)

Word origin: Greek transliteration of Hebrew Yay-shoo-ah יֵשׁוּעַ, short form of Y'ho-shoo-ah, יְהוֹשׁוּעַ meaning "YHVH is salvation."

(This card is from the final flashcard set of Book 2)

temple, sanctuary, holy place

Word origin: from a primary word, an adjective ἱερός, meaning "sacred"

(This card is from the final flashcard set of Book 2)

world, universe, the earth, order (i.e., an ordered system, like the order of creation); *by extension,* all humankind

Word origin: a primary word

(This card is from the final flashcard set of Book 2)

the "heart" – i.e., inner life, mind, inner self, character, intention, will, seat of life.

Word origin: a primary word. Note that in scripture, it is never once used to refer to the physical organ in the body that pumps blood.

(This card is from the final flashcard set of Book 2)

κύριος, -ου, ὁ

masculine noun, second declension

nom sg	κύριος	nom pl	κύριοι
gen sg	κυρίου	gen pl	κυρίων
dat sg	κυρίῳ	dat pl	κυρίοις
acc sg	κύριον	acc pl	κυρίους
voc sg	κύριε	voc pl	κύριοι

λόγος, -ου, ὁ

masculine noun, second declension

nom sg	λόγος	nom pl	λόγοι
gen sg	λόγου	gen pl	λόγων
dat sg	λόγῳ	dat pl	λόγοις
acc sg	λόγον	acc pl	λόγους
voc sg	λόγε	voc pl	λόγοι

μαθητής, -οῦ, ὁ

masculine noun, first declension

nom sg	μαθητής	nom pl	μαθηταί
gen sg	μαθητοῦ	gen pl	μαθητῶν
dat sg	μαθητῇ	dat pl	μαθηταῖς
acc sg	μαθητήν	acc pl	μαθητάς
voc sg	μαθητά	voc pl	μαθηταί

νόμος, -ου, ὁ

masculine noun, second declension

nom sg	νόμος	nom pl	νόμοι
gen sg	νόμου	gen pl	νόμων
dat sg	νόμῳ	dat pl	νόμοις
acc sg	νόμον	acc pl	νόμους
voc sg	νόμε	voc pl	νόμοι

ὁ, ἡ, τό

	masc	fem	neut		masc	fem	neut
nom sg	ὁ	ἡ	τό	nom pl	οἱ	αἱ	τά
gen sg	τοῦ	τῆς	τοῦ	gen pl	τῶν	τῶν	τῶν
dat sg	τῷ	τῇ	τῷ	dat pl	τοῖς	ταῖς	τοῖς
acc sg	τόν	τήν	τό	acc pl	τούς	τάς	τά
voc sg	ὦ	ὦ	ὦ	voc pl	ὦ	ὦ	ὦ

ὄνομα, -ματος, τό

neuter noun, third declension

nom sg	ὄνομα	nom pl	ὀνόματα
gen sg	ὀνόματος	gen pl	ὀνομάτων
dat sg	ὀνόματι	dat pl	ὀνόμασι(ν)
acc sg	ὄνομα	acc pl	ὀνόματα
voc sg	ὄνομα	voc pl	ὀνόματα

οὐρανός, -οῦ, ὁ

masculine noun, second declension

nom sg	οὐρανός	nom pl	οὐρανοί
gen sg	οὐρανοῦ	gen pl	οὐρανῶν
dat sg	οὐρανῷ	dat pl	οὐρανοῖς
acc sg	οὐρανόν	acc pl	οὐρανούς
voc sg	οὐρανέ	voc pl	οὐρανοί

πατήρ, πατρός, ὁ

masculine noun, third declension

nom sg	πατήρ	nom pl	πατέρες
gen sg	πατρός	gen pl	πατέρων
dat sg	πατρί	dat pl	πατράσι(ν)
acc sg	πατέρα	acc pl	πατέρας
voc sg	πάτερ	voc pl	πατέρες

πίστις, πίστεως, ἡ

feminine noun, third declension

nom sg	πίστις	nom pl	unused
gen sg	πίστεως	gen pl	unused
dat sg	πίστει	dat pl	unused
acc sg	πίστιν	acc pl	unused
voc sg	unused	voc pl	unused

πνεῦμα, -ατος, τό

neuter noun, third declension

nom sg	πνεῦμα	nom pl	πνεύματα
gen sg	πνεύματος	gen pl	πνευμάτων
dat sg	πνεύματι	dat pl	πνεύμασι(ν)
acc sg	πνεῦμα	acc pl	πνεύματα
voc sg	πνεῦμα	voc pl	πνεύματα

a word (or thought), speech, divine utterance, human statement/communication; a reasoning, accounting, reckoning, doctrine or narrative

Word origin: from a primary verb λέγω *"to speak," originally meaning "to lay to rest," i.e., to move a message or an argument toward its conclusion*

(This card is from the final flashcard set of Book 2)

---

lord, Lord, master, sir, one who exercises authority with full rights of ownership

Word origin: from κῦρος *"supremacy," originally meaning "to be strong, to prevail." In ancient usage, it denoted a master exercising ownership.*

(This card is from the final flashcard set of Book 2)

---

a law, "the Law" (of God) or a general principle; a custom, precept, that which is assigned or established by usage

Word origin: from a primary verb νέμω *"to distribute, parcel out, apportion or assign"*

(This card is from the final flashcard set of Book 2)

---

a learner, disciple, pupil

Word origin: from the same root as μανθάνω *"to learn" by increasing in knowledge, by being trained in instruction; to gain new habits by use and practice*

(This card is from the final flashcard set of Book 2)

---

name, character/reputation, fame, authority ("in the name of")

Word origin: a primary word

(This card is from the final flashcard set of Book 2)

The Greek article

Often translated "<u>the</u>," the article may also be translated *of, to, who/whom, that/what/which, one, some, all, those who, whoever,* etc. depending on context. There are times it is not translated into English at all, as when it appears before proper nouns or would be incorrect to do so in English.

---

a father, the (Heavenly) Father; an ancestor; *respectful address of an older man:* elder, senior, teacher; *figuratively:* an author, founder or originator

Word origin: a primary word

(This card is from the final flashcard set of Book 2)

---

heaven, the heavens, the vaulted sky, the physical atmosphere and stars above it (equivalent to the universe), the spiritual heavens (God's dwelling place)

Word origin: a primary word

(This card is from the final flashcard set of Book 2)

---

spirit, the (Holy) Spirit, wind, breath

Word origin: from a primary verb πνέω *"to blow, to breathe" (as the wind)*

(This card is from the final flashcard set of Book 2)

---

trust, faith, belief, confidence; fidelity, faithfulness

Word origin: from a primary verb πείθω *"to persuade, to be persuaded" (of what is trustworthy). Faith is a gift from God (1 Cor. 12:9); He <u>persuades</u> the believer that He is indeed trustworthy.*

(This card is from the final flashcard set of Book 2)

πρόσωπον, -ου, τό

neuter noun, second declension

nom sg	πρόσωπον	nom pl	πρόσωπα
gen sg	προσώπου	gen pl	προσώπων
dat sg	προσώπῳ	dat pl	προσώποις
acc sg	πρόσωπον	acc pl	πρόσωπα
voc sg	πρόσωπον	voc pl	πρόσωπα

σάρξ, σαρκός, ἡ

feminine noun, third declension

nom sg	σάρξ	nom pl	σάρκες
gen sg	σαρκός	gen pl	σαρκῶν
dat sg	σαρκί	dat pl	σαρξί(ν)
acc sg	σάρκα	acc pl	σάρκας
voc sg	σάρξ	voc pl	σάρκες

σημεῖον, -ου, τό

neuter noun, second declension

nom sg	σημεῖον	nom pl	σημεῖα
gen sg	σημείου	gen pl	σημείων
dat sg	σημείῳ	dat pl	σημείοις
acc sg	σημεῖον	acc pl	σημεῖα
voc sg	σημεῖον	voc pl	σημεῖα

τέκνον, -ου, τό

neuter noun, second declension

nom sg	τέκνον	nom pl	τέκνα
gen sg	τέκνου	gen pl	τέκνων
dat sg	τέκνῳ	dat pl	τέκνοις
acc sg	τέκνον	acc pl	τέκνα
voc sg	τέκνον	voc pl	τέκνα

υἱός, -οῦ, ὁ

masculine noun, second declension

nom sg	υἱός	nom pl	υἱοί
gen sg	υἱοῦ	gen pl	υἱῶν
dat sg	υἱῷ	dat pl	υἱοῖς
acc sg	υἱόν	acc pl	υἱούς
voc sg	υἱέ	voc pl	υἱοί

φωνή, -ῆς, ἡ

feminine noun, first declension

nom sg	φωνή	nom pl	φωναί
gen sg	φωνῆς	gen pl	φωνῶν
dat sg	φωνῇ	dat pl	φωναῖς
acc sg	φωνήν	acc pl	φωνάς
voc sg	φωνή	voc pl	φωναί

χάρις, -ιτος, ἡ

feminine noun, third declension

nom sg	χάρις	nom pl	χάριτες
gen sg	χάριτος	gen pl	χαρίτων
dat sg	χάριτι	dat pl	χάρισι(ν)
acc sg	χάριτα/χάριν	acc pl	χάριτας
voc sg	χάρις	voc pl	χάριτες

Χριστός, -οῦ, ὁ

masculine noun, second declension

nom sg	Χριστός	nom pl	unused
gen sg	Χριστοῦ	gen pl	unused
dat sg	Χριστῷ	dat pl	unused
acc sg	Χριστόν	acc pl	unused
voc sg	Χριστέ	voc pl	unused

ψυχή, -ῆς, ἡ

feminine noun, first declension

nom sg	ψυχή	nom pl	ψυχαί
gen sg	ψυχῆς	gen pl	ψυχῶν
dat sg	ψυχῇ	dat pl	ψυχαῖς
acc sg	ψυχήν	acc pl	ψυχάς
voc sg	ψυχή	voc pl	ψυχαί

flesh, body, human nature, materiality, physical kin (*"brothers after the flesh"*), of natural, animal or human origin as opposed to spiritual origin

Word origin: a primary word

(This card is from the final flashcard set of Book 2)

---

the face, visage, countenance (*by extension,* surface, appearance)

Word origin: from a preposition πρός *"towards"* + *a primary root* οπ *"to see"*

(This card is from the final flashcard set of Book 2)

---

a child (either male or female), a descendant; an inhabitant or dependent (*"children of that city"*); one begotten physically or spiritually (*"child of God"*)

Word origin: from a verb τίκτω *"to beget, bring forth, produce, bear, yield"*

(This card is from the final flashcard set of Book 2)

---

a sign, typically miraculous; a mark, token, indication which confirms or authenticates

Word origin: from the same as σημαίνω *"to signify, give a sign, make known, indicate"*

(This card is from the final flashcard set of Book 2)

---

voice, noise, sound; *by extension,* language, dialect, utterance

Word origin: of uncertain origin

(This card is from the final flashcard set of Book 2)

---

son (by birth or by adoption), descendant; in scripture (*figuratively*) anyone sharing the same nature as his father

Word origin: a primary word

(This card is from the final flashcard set of Book 2)

The Anointed One (Messiah), the Christ; (*when not capitalized*) an anointed one

Word origin: from a verb χρίω *"to anoint by rubbing or pouring olive oil on someone"* representing someone as divinely appointed to serve as a prophet, priest or king, etc.

(This card is from the final flashcard set of Book 2)

---

grace, favor, kindness; often in scripture refers to God's leaning/reaching toward man to extend benefit

Word origin: a primary word

(This card is from the final flashcard set of Book 2)

---

the soul, life, self; the vital breath; the seat of affections and will, the mind; a human person, an individual

Word origin: of uncertain origin.

(This card is from the final flashcard set of Book 2)

Congratulations!

Congratulations! You have completed Book 2 of *Biblical Greek!*

Let's take a moment to thank God for helping us arrive at this point. *"Thank you, Jesus, for helping us learn a little more about the Greek language. Help us now to apply the things we learn in Your Word in our daily lives. Amen."*

We just wanted to remind you that, at the very end of this book, there is a glossary containing all of the words in the flashcards on the preceding pages, so don't be afraid to cut out all the flashcards and begin using them. Enjoy!

Where do you go from here?

Keep an eye out for other books in this series. We're working as hard as we can to provide you with all the tools you will need to "rightly divide the Word of truth." Each year, we try to add more titles, to give you a real fighting chance in your pursuit of Biblical languages.

For a list of some of the other books we have already released, see the pages immediately following. We have many other books in progress. The moment they are completed, we'll make them available through the same online book retailers from whom you purchased this book. So, every once in a while, just take a minute and do a quick search under the author names "James and Lisa Cummins" to see what's new out there!

Grace and peace be yours in abundance through the knowledge of God and of Jesus our Lord (2 Pet. 1:2).

– Jim and Lisa

Other Books
by James T. and Lisa M. Cummins

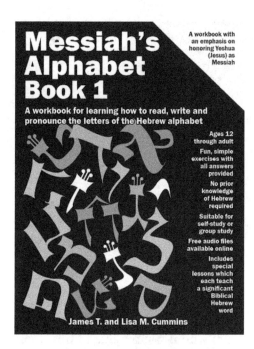

Messiah's Alphabet Book 1: A workbook for learning how to read, write and pronounce the letters of the Hebrew alphabet

The first book in the *Messiah's Alphabet* series introduces the Hebrew alphabet to those with no prior knowledge of Hebrew. The student is shown how to draw simple "stick figure" shapes for each letter, and then learns the sound and name of each letter in a fun and friendly manner. The book gradually introduces some of the most frequently used Hebrew words in the Bible, gently assisting the reader in learning to recognize and pronounce each one. Audio files of every lesson available.

Available now through online book retailers

Messiah's Alphabet Book 2: Building a Biblical Vocabulary

The second book in the *Messiah's Alphabet* series, this workbook teaches basic Hebrew grammar on topics such as the definite article "the", the conjunction "and," plural nouns, adjectives and possessives for singular nouns. Guided readings of short scripture passages are included throughout. Fun, simple exercises with all answers are provided. Puzzles, riddles and tear-out "flashcard" pages are included. Intended for students who have completed Book 1 or who have a solid working knowledge of the Hebrew alphabet and are able to phonetically "sound out" Hebrew words. Audio files of every lesson available.

Available now through online book retailers

Other Books by James T. and Lisa M. Cummins, *continued*

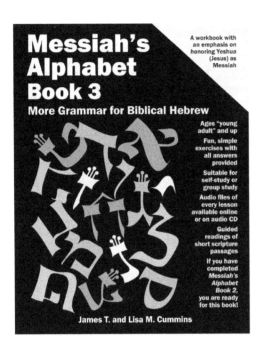

Messiah's Alphabet Book 3: More Grammar for Biblical Hebrew
The third book in the *Messiah's Alphabet* series covers topics such as participles, prepositions (standalone and inseparable), prepositions with pronominal suffixes, and construct chains (word pairs). Each lesson introduces plenty of new Biblical Hebrew vocabulary. Continuing in the same fun and friendly style as the other books in the series, the workbook contains cartoons, jokes, puzzles, flashcard pages, and answers to all exercises. Audio files of vocabulary from every lesson are available.

Available now through online book retailers

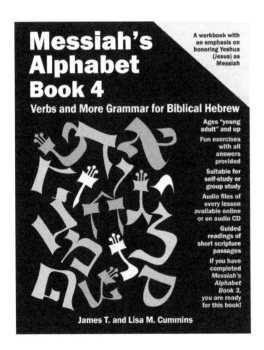

Messiah's Alphabet Book 4: Verbs and More Grammar for Biblical Hebrew
The fourth book in the *Messiah's Alphabet* series covers verbs (roots, past tense, future tense, imperative and infinitive), the direct object marker, possessive suffixes for plural nouns, and the reversing *vav*. Each lesson introduces new Biblical Hebrew vocabulary. Continuing in the same fun and friendly style as the other books in the series, the workbook contains cartoons, jokes, puzzles, flashcard pages, and answers to all exercises. The book also includes Verb Charts, which give conjugations of frequently used verbs. Audio files of all newly introduced vocabulary are available.

Available now through online book retailers

Other Books by James T. and Lisa M. Cummins, *continued*

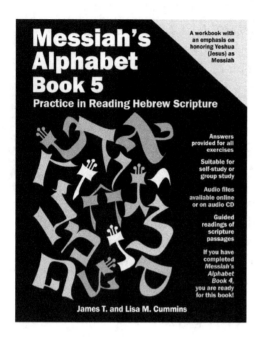

Messiah's Alphabet Book 5: Practice in Reading Hebrew Scripture allows the student who has completed Books 1 through 4 of the series to spread his or her wings and practice reading entire passages of scripture, using mostly the vocabulary already taught in the series. Some new vocabulary is taught in this book, too, including tear-out flashcard pages, verb charts and glossary. Comparison tables of Christian, traditional Jewish and Messianic translations for every passage are included. Intriguing discussion questions explore selected Hebrew phrases. Complete answer keys with grammatical notations included. Emphasis on Yeshua (Jesus) as Savior and LORD. Audio files of every lesson available.

Available now through online book retailers

"But WAIT... There's more!
See the next pages!"

- Jim and Lisa

Other Books by James T. and Lisa M. Cummins, *continued*

Messiah's Alphabet: Names Have Meaning is an exploration into the actual Hebrew meanings of the names of certain people mentioned in the Bible. Surprising discoveries will unfold as you connect the true meaning of each Hebrew name with its prophetic significance and fulfillment in scripture. The hidden Hebrew meanings underlying the names of New Testament people are also brought to light. While a basic knowledge of the Hebrew and Greek alphabets may be helpful, it is not necessary, as all pronunciations are provided in transliteration form using the letters of the English alphabet. All answers are provided in the text. Audio files of every lesson available.

Available now through online book retailers

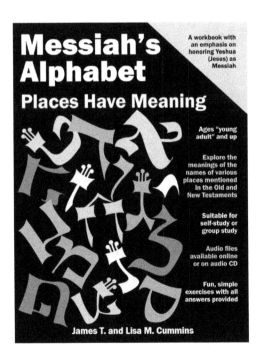

Messiah's Alphabet: Places Have Meaning is an exploration into the actual Hebrew meanings of the names of certain places mentioned in the Bible. Surprising discoveries will unfold as you connect the true meaning of each Hebrew name with its prophetic significance and fulfillment in scripture. The hidden Hebrew meanings underlying the names of New Testament places are also brought to light. While a basic knowledge of the Hebrew and Greek alphabets may be helpful, it is not necessary, as all pronunciations are provided in transliteration form using the letters of the English alphabet. All answers are provided in the text. Audio files of every lesson available.

Available now through online book retailers

God invented a calendar. Now, you can learn all about it!

Did any New Testament events align with God's special "appointed times" of the Old Testament?

How do God's Old Testament holy days act as prophetic "pictures" of future things to come?

How does knowing the order of the Biblical months help clarify the order of events in the New Testament?

Did you know that certain historical events tend to recur during certain months in the Biblical calendar – such as the destructions of *both* the first and second temples, which occurred more than 600 years apart, but on the *same date*?

Don't worry if you've never heard of a Biblical calendar before... *Messiah's Calendar Book 1: Days, Weeks, Months and Years* offers a gentle introduction to the concepts of Biblical timekeeping, God's calendar, and God's appointed times, with an emphasis on their ultimate fulfillment in Messiah Jesus (Yeshua). Learn about God's definitions of the day, the week, the month and the year. Get familiar with the order of the Biblical months and see how it helps clarify the order of events in your New Testament. This book's educational illustrations and excellent graphics - packed with prophetic insights and historical information - make God's calendar easy to grasp. The writing style and choice of vocabulary are sensitive to both Jewish and Gentile readers, so this book is suitable for churches and Messianic congregations alike.

Other great features include:

- **Educational illustrations throughout**

- **Packed with Biblical insights**

- **Listed scriptures are fully "typed out" for convenience in classroom study**

- **Brief descriptions of all feasts and fasts**

- **Easy explanations of any Hebrew or Greek terms, with simple phonetic pronunciations. (Prior knowledge of Hebrew or Greek is not necessary.)**

- **Additional resources in the back, including graphics, teachings and glossary/index**

- **Excellent for either group or individual study**

Nisan / Abib

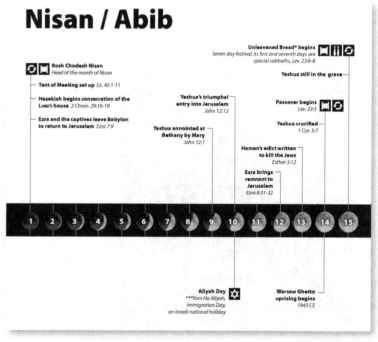

You'll enjoy the clear, easy to use graphics – portraying the date of every event mentioned in scripture... as well as the dates of key historical events which are not mentioned in the Bible.

Other Books by James T. and Lisa M. Cummins, *continued*

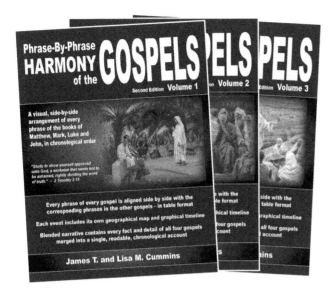

Phrase-By-Phrase Harmony of the Gospels – This is a visual, side-by-side arrangement of every phrase of the books of Matthew, Mark, Luke and John, in chronological order. Every phrase of every gospel is aligned side by side with the corresponding phrases in the other gospels, in table format. Each event includes its own geographical map and graphical timeline. Blended narrative contains every fact and detail of all four gospels, merged into a single, readable, chronological account.

Available now through online book retailers

Modular design: Focus your attention on one event per section.

Graphical Timeline on every section: Keep track of what happened before and what's coming up.

Phrase-By-Phrase Harmonized Table: Compare every phrase of scripture from all four gospels at a glance. Bolded and italicized typefaces indicate time and geography references.

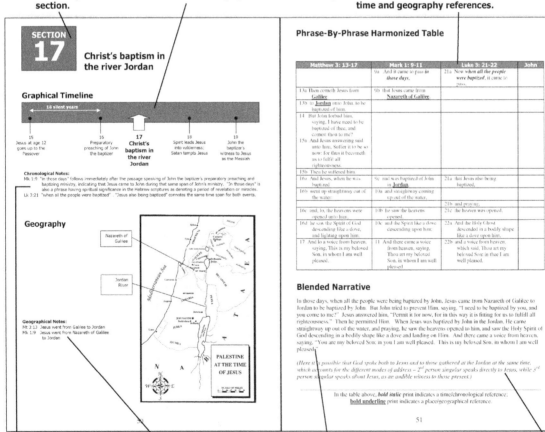

Chronological Notes: Insightful commentary on the historical or cultural significance of all time references.

Geographical Notes with Map on every section: Keep track of where each event occurs. Historical and archaeological notes are provided wherever applicable.

Blended Narrative: This account, in readable modern language, contains every factual detail of all four gospels, in chronological order.

Authors' Commentary is provided wherever clarification of difficult or problematic texts is necessary.

Novels by James T. and Lisa M. Cummins

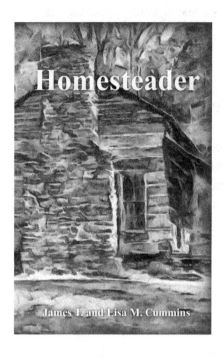

Homesteader

It's 1957, and thirteen-year-old Jimmy dreams of homesteading a piece of land just like he's seen the pioneers do on his favorite TV show. As soon as he finds the perfect spot to build a homestead, he gets caught trespassing on an old man's property. It's just the first of many hard lessons about the realities of life. After years of hard work and patience, Jimmy gradually begins to have some success. Throughout life's tragedies and triumphs, he learns the value of enduring friendship.

Available now through online book retailers

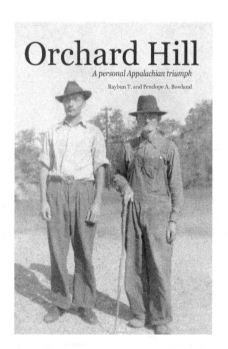

Orchard Hill

It is a time of extreme economic desperation. When Raybun returns to the Kentucky homeplace after fighting in the Second World War, he is dismayed to discover the entire region suffering in extreme poverty resulting from economic changes beyond anyone's control. Now, Raybun must find a way to help his family and community. Through a series of small miracles and a growing, persistent faith, Raybun and his friends are able to bring restoration to the broken community, and find love along the way.

Available now through online book retailers under author names James T. and Lisa M. Cummins and pseudonyms Raybun and Penelope Bowland

Glossary

ἀδελφός, -οῦ, ὁ — brother; *figuratively,* member of the same religious community (fellow believer). *Word origin:* α + δελφύς *(womb),* "one/same womb"

ἁμαρτία, -ας, ἡ — sin, moral failure/offense, ethical fault, sinful deed or thought. *Word origin: from the root of* ἁμαρτάνω, *"to miss, to fail"*

ἀνήρ, ἀνδρός, ὁ — man (adult male human being), husband. *Word origin: a primary word*

ἄνθρωπος, -ου, ὁ — man (male), mankind (male and female), humanity, human being, person. *Word origin uncertain, possibly from* ἀνήρ

ἄρχων, -οντος, ὁ — ruler, prince, leader, chief. (Within first-century Judaism, an official member of the assembly of elders.) *Word origin: from the present participle of* ἄρχω, *"to rule, take precedence, begin, start"*

βασιλεία, -ας, ἡ — kingdom, dominion, sovereignty, rule, kingly authority. Esp. of God, both concretely and in the hearts of men. *Word origin: from the stem of* βασιλεύς, *"king"*

γῆ, γῆς, ἡ — earth, soil/arable land, mainland, region (i.e., a territory and its inhabitants). *Word origin: a primary word*

γυνή, γυναικός, ἡ — woman, wife. *Word origin: a primary word*

ἐλπίς, -ίδος, ἡ — hope, expectation, trust, confidence (in the certainty of that which is to come). *Word origin: from the same as* ἐλπίζω, *"to hope with anticipation or expectation"*

ἔργον, -ου, τό — work, labor, action, deed, that which is wrought or made, something accomplished which carries out an intention or purpose. *Word origin: from a primary (obsolete) verb "to work"*

εὐαγγέλιον, -ου, τό — good news, the gospel; specifically, the glad tidings of the kingdom of God throughout Old and New Testaments. *Word origin: from same as* εὐαγγελίζω, *from* εὖ *"good, well"* + ἄγγελος *"angel, messenger"; i.e., "good message"*

Glossary, *continued*

ζωή, -ῆς, ἡ   life (spiritual or physical). *Word origin: from* ζῶ, *"to live"*

ἡμέρα, -ας, ἡ   day (daylight, as contrasted with night); or the civil day (in Judaism, the 24 hours beginning at sunset and concluding with the following sunset); or that prophesied "Day" in which the Lord shall judge men. *Word origin: a primary word*

θεός, -οῦ, ὁ   God, a god. *Word origin uncertain*

ἱερόν, -οῦ, τό   temple, sanctuary, holy place. *Word origin: from a primary word, an adjective* ἱερός, *meaning "sacred"*

Ἰησοῦς, -οῦ, ὁ   Jesus, i.e. Joshua (Hebrew, *Yeshua*, a short form of the Hebrew name *Yehoshua*). *Word origin: Greek transliteration of Hebrew Yay-shoo-ah,* יֵשׁוּעַ *, short form of Y'ho-shoo-ah,* יְהוֹשׁוּעַ *, meaning "YHVH is salvation."*

καρδία, -ας, ἡ   the "heart" – i.e., inner life, mind, inner self, character, intention, will, seat of life. *Word origin: a primary word. Note that in scripture, it is never once used to refer to the physical organ in the body that pumps blood.*

κόσμος, -ου, ὁ   world, universe, the earth, order (i.e., an ordered system, like the order of creation); *by extension,* all humankind. *Word origin: a primary word*

κύριος, -ου, ὁ   lord, Lord, master, sir, one who exercises authority with full rights of ownership. *Word origin: from* κῦρος *"supremacy," originally meaning "to be strong, to prevail." In ancient usage, it denoted a master exercising ownership.*

λόγος, -ου, ὁ   a word (or thought), speech, divine utterance, human statement/ communication; a reasoning, accounting, reckoning, doctrine or narrative. *Word origin: from a primary verb* λέγω *"to speak," originally meaning "to lay to rest," i.e., to move a message or an argument toward its conclusion*

μαθητής, -οῦ, ὁ   a learner, disciple, pupil. *Word origin: from the same root as* μανθάνω *"to learn" by increasing in knowledge, by being trained in instruction; to gain new habits by use and practice*

Glossary, *continued*

νόμος, -ου, ὁ   a law, "the Law" (of God) or a general principle; a custom, precept, that which is assigned or established by usage. *Word origin: from a primary verb* νέμω *"to distribute, parcel out, apportion or assign"*

ὁ, ἡ, τό   the Greek article. Often translated "<u>the</u>," the article may also be translated *of the, to the, who/whom, that/what/which, one, some, all, those who, whoever,* etc. depending on context. There are times it is not translated into English at all, as when it appears before proper nouns or would be otherwise incorrect to do so in English.

ὄνομα, -ματος, τό   name, character/reputation, fame, authority ("in the name of"). *Word origin: a primary word*

οὐρανός, -οῦ, ὁ   heaven, the heavens, the vaulted sky, the physical atmosphere and stars above it (equivalent to the universe), the spiritual heavens (God's dwelling place). *Word origin: a primary word*

πατήρ, πατρός, ὁ   a father, the (Heavenly) Father; an ancestor; *respectful address of an older man:* elder, senior, teacher; *figuratively:* an author, founder or originator. *Word origin: a primary word*

πίστις, πίστεως, ἡ   trust, faith, belief, confidence; fidelity, faithfulness. *Word origin: from a primary verb* πείθω *"to persuade, to be persuaded" (of what is trustworthy). Faith is a gift from God (1 Cor. 12:9); He* <u>persuades</u> *the believer that He is indeed trustworthy.*

πνεῦμα, -ατος, τό   spirit, the (Holy) Spirit, wind, breath. *Word origin: from a primary verb* πνέω *"to blow, to breathe" (as the wind)*

πρόσωπον, -ου, τό   the face, visage, countenance (*by extension,* surface, appearance). *Word origin: from a preposition* πρός *"towards" + a primary root* οπ *"to see"*

σάρξ, σαρκός, ἡ   flesh, body, human nature, materiality, physical kin (*"brothers after the flesh"*), of natural, animal or human origin as opposed to spiritual origin. *Word origin: a primary word*

Glossary, *continued*

σημεῖον, -ου, τό — a sign, typically miraculous; a mark, token, indication which confirms or authenticates. *Word origin: from the same as* σημαίνω *"to signify, give a sign, make known, indicate"*

τέκνον, -ου, τό — a child (either male or female), a descendant; an inhabitant or dependent *("children of that city")*; one begotten physically or spiritually *("child of God")*. *Word origin: from a verb* τίκτω *"to beget, bring forth, produce, bear, yield"*

υἱός, -οῦ, ὁ — son (by birth or by adoption), descendant; in scripture *(figuratively)* anyone sharing the same nature as his father. *Word origin: a primary word*

φωνή, -ῆς, ἡ — voice, noise, sound; *by extension*, language, dialect, utterance. *Word origin: of uncertain origin*

χάρις, -ιτος, ἡ — grace, favor, kindness; often in scripture refers to God's leaning/reaching toward man to extend benefit. *Word origin: a primary word*

Χριστός, -οῦ, ὁ — The Anointed One (Messiah), the Christ; *(when not capitalized)* an anointed one. *Word origin: from a verb* χρίω *"to anoint by rubbing or pouring olive oil on someone" representing someone as divinely appointed to serve as a prophet, priest or king, etc.*

ψυχή, -ῆς, ἡ — the soul, life, self; the vital breath; the seat of affections and will, the mind; a human person, an individual. *Word origin: of uncertain origin.*

CPSIA information can be obtained
at www.ICGtesting.com
Printed in the USA
LVHW102318300919
632803LV00009B/227/P